THE
O.J.
SYNDROME

Confessions of an Abuser

by Rich Bean

with Karen Crane

THE O.J. SYNDROME

BLUE BIRD PUBLISHING
1739 East Broadway #306
Tempe AZ 85282
(602) 968-4088 (602) 831-6063

Printed in the United States of America
ISBN 0-933025-39-4 $11.95
Cover Art by Rob D. Wipprecht

Library of Congress Cataloguing in Publication Data
Bean, Richard, 1938-
    The O.J. syndrome : confessions of an abuser /
by Richard Bean, with Karen Crane.
      p. cm.
    Includes bibliographical references.
    ISBN 0-933025-39-4
    1. Abusive men--United States--Case Studies. 2.
Abusive men--Rehabilitation--United States--Case
studies. 3. Wife abuse--United States--Christianity.
4. Wife abuse--Religious aspects--Christianity.
  I. Crane, Karen, 1962-   II. Title.
HV6626.2.B43   1995
306.872--dc20
                                95-16615
                                   CIP

To Ginnie, the wonderful person who put up with me for all of those years and gave me many, many second chances.

Contents

Preface

This book contains the story of my abusive marriage along with some of the things I have learned over a long journey. I have been married to the same woman for almost forty years, but I often refer to my "first wife" and my "first marriage" because of the radical difference in our relationship now as compared to what it was fifteen years ago.

It has been very emotionally exhausting for me to write this book. To do so, I have had to relive some difficult and traumatic moments in my life, situations I would rather forget about and things that I have pushed to the back corner of my mind. But in order for others to benefit from my experience, it was necessary to dig up the truth, no matter how ugly it all is. So, that is why I am bearing my soul and exposing it to all of the world—with the hope that it will benefit someone else.

Only as I write this book have I come to grips with the fact that I was an abusive husband. Until I started to put my story down on paper, I had never realized this. I always thought I was just a man who wanted his own way. I guess it's because I really do love my wife that I couldn't see myself as an abuser, but I know now that's exactly what I was.

I cannot help but wonder how many other men

are in that same place in their relationships—knowing that something is wrong but not able to face the reality that they are abusers and, even if they realize it, not being able to do anything about it. I also wonder if I will be able to get my message through to them, especially when I consider how hard it was to face it myself.

My hope is to make at least some small difference in the lives of others caught in the trap of abuse. It is a trap where none of the prisoners will likely get out unharmed. Like any other difficulty in life, the first step to resolution is recognizing that the problem exists and having a true desire to conquer it. I feel very strongly that this book can be the true launching pad for any man who has the problem and is at the point in his life where he wants to do something about it.

For me, my deep faith in God was the reason I was able to change from a life of abuse to a life of love. But this is not a religious book. I believe that any man can relate to the message it contains, no matter what his beliefs. But I also know that I could not have gotten where I am today if it weren't for the unfailing love and forgiveness of my Lord.

For those of you who have the abusive kind of relationship (or think you might), my story should show you a little light at the end of that dark, depressing tunnel to nowhere. And even if you are not an abuser, you can still improve the quality of the relationship you have by using the principles in this book.

There is a tendency for some to believe that the

It's time for us to
do something about
the "O.J. Syndrome."

problem will get better with age, or that we abusers will "outgrow" the problem. I wish that were true, but it's not that simple. My problem only got worse as time went by. That's how it is for most of us who don't get help.

In fact, my father, who started the pattern of abuse in my family by abusing my mother all of their married life, died without ever changing his ways. Only a short time before my father passed away, my brother had to remove the pistol my father kept under his bed. He was threatening to shoot my mother and her "friend." She was 72 at the time. No such male friend had ever existed.

I have chosen the title "The O.J. Syndrome" for this book, and I believe that this problem is much more common today than we may realize. If we can name the problem, perhaps we can then begin to solve it.

It's time for us to do something about the "O.J. Syndrome."

The O.J. Syndrome

Introduction

My wife, Ginnie, and I just got back from a three day trip to Disney World. We've been many times before, but this time was different. This time the best part of the trip was not the entertainment. It was the deep harmony and joy we had in each other's company. We didn't fight or argue. We didn't accuse and blame each other for anything. We did, however, joke, laugh, and love a lot. And we savored every single moment.

But it hasn't always been this way. There was a time in our relationship when we could not be together for more than a few hours without fighting and arguing. We were caught in an abusive relationship that was going nowhere.

I was an abuser.

I admit to having been one, but I am far from alone. In the United States, every 12 seconds a woman is battered and every year more than 4,000 women die from injuries administered by someone who supposedly loves them. That's hard for most people to understand.

We don't even know how many millions more are beaten and live. Instead of dying, they suffer, usually all alone. It is a crime of secrecy. I certainly kept it a secret. Many women never report abuse for the sake of their children or for fear of what their tormentor will do to them if they seek help.

Ironically, the men who abuse suffer too. For many years, I suffered, knowing deep down inside of me that Ginnie was losing her love for me. I just didn't know what to do about it. And I didn't realize that I was the cause of it.

Those of us who treat women with such disrespect know what we want. We want for our women to love us more than they love anyone else. We want them to submit to our authority. But we don't know how to make them do those things, so we strike out in the only way we know. We become physical, we become abusive.

Yet in our own way, those of us who abuse really do love the women we hurt. We love them in the only way we know. We love them wildly, irrationally,

---

Those of us who treat women with such disrespect know what we want. We want for our women to love us more than they love anyone else. We want them to submit to our authority. But we don't know how to make them do those things, so we strike out in the only way we know. We become physical, we become abusive.

---

and possessively. And in the end, our kind of love hurts them.

I loved my wife, but we who abuse try to control, we try to dominate, we try to make the ones we love different, into what we think we want them to be.

The reality is that people don't marry another person. They marry an ideal— an image of what they expect the other person to be. But a real life person may never live up to a fantasized image. Being human makes us all independent. To make matters worse, I believe that the facts show that men just don't understand women and how they think. And so the conflict begins.

If you are an abuser, you simply try harder and harder to force the person you love to become like the image you have in your mind, even at the expense of her own well-being. <u>And in the end, you don't like what you create.</u> Love and trust never come out of hurt and abuse. Unfortunately, I had to find that out the hard way. What Ginnie and I had was not a love relationship but more like the relationship of a master-slave.

Personally, I believe that the problem of abuse is solely a gender issue. It is a kind of discrimination against women. I am resolute in my belief that it is man versus woman, male versus female, and nothing more.

And what about the other victims of this tragedy—the children? Children today have so much to deal with in our society as it is. Abuse of their mother at home only adds to their hardship. And there is never the guarantee that they won't become victims of abuse

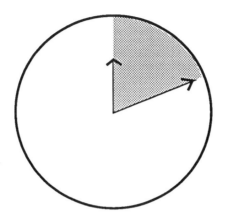

Every 12 seconds a woman is battered.

It is estimated that as many as 4,000 women die each year at the hands of their domestic partners.

75% of women killed by the man they love are killed while trying to leave.

72% of men who beat their wives eventually beat their children.

For information packet on domestic violence, write: National Coalition Against Domestic Violence, PO Box 18749, Denver CO 80218-0749.

themselves. Illustrating this point, CBS evening news reported on September 23, 1994 that seventy-two percent of men who beat their wives will eventually beat their children.

Author Sylvia Ann Hewlett, in her article "Tough Choice, Great Rewards," explains, "It takes enormous amounts of energy and time to raise children, and all of us must understand the trade-offs between personal fulfillment and family well-being." But when the parents are engaged in an emotional life and death struggle with each other, where will the energy and time to give to the children come from? It just won't be there.

Then why do we do it? Why does an abuser continue to bully and control the one he loves when all that he is creating is a deepening hatred within her and a gnawing pain in the pit of his own stomach? Up until 1984, I didn't know the answer to that question. I do now. Today, after nearly 40 years of marriage, Ginnie and I are happy together and have a great relationship.

In this book I will tell you my story and how it all changed for me.

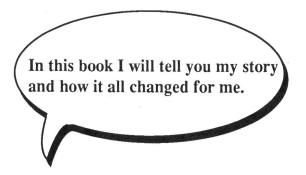

- 1 -

The O.J. Syndrome Defined

Webster defines a syndrome as "a set of concurrent things such as emotions or actions that usually form an identifiable pattern." In my case, my behavior toward my wife formed an identifiable pattern—a syndrome. It was a pattern of anger and of regular abuse. I call it the O.J. syndrome, but I could just as easily have called it the Rich Bean Syndrome or any number of thousands of other names, maybe even yours. I know that this syndrome is shared by many men—perhaps millions—in the United States.

Exactly what are the behaviors that characterized this syndrome? How do you recognize if you are living it? From my experience, there are two very recognizable indicators to look for—jealousy and a need to control.

1. Jealousy

Most people have experienced jealousy at some time in their lives, probably many times. The abusive person, however, feels a jealousy that is much more intense and is triggered by events that are often only imagined in his mind—a hidden fear of losing the one he loves. For instance, he may not want his wife to go out without him in the evening, even if it is just with some female friends, because he fears that she will meet some other man while she is out. Or he may fly into a rage if he sees her chatting with another man, even though there is no basis for the anger and the conversation is completely innocent.

He may even be jealous of her friendships with other women because he worries that she will become too intimate with them, taking away from the intimacy that he demands from her with himself. He may also imagine that her relationships with other women will somehow lead her into an encounter with another man.

Over time, his jealousy will become a prison for her. She will not be able to have girlfriends because he fears they will take her attention away from him. She almost certainly will not be allowed to have any male friends. In short, her social life becomes only what he allows her to have and then only when he is present. She will not be permitted to be away from him for very long periods of time, unless it is to go to work. Even trips to the grocery become suspect. He may question why it would take so long for her to shop for food, picturing in his mind all of the men she is secretly seeing during this time when she's supposed to be shopping.

If you don't know this "Green-Eyed Monster" then I am happy for you. You see, he is a tormentor who shares your existence. He only sleeps when you do and sometimes even finds his way into your dreams, especially your daydreams. He is always whispering to you that your woman is looking for someone else and that she surely has a male friend who is really more than a friend, a lover.

He tells you to look for evidence everywhere, and by all means to keep your eyes open. "Check her purse, come home unexpectedly, call to see if she is really at work, check up on her any way you can," he will say. Any time she rejects your advances for any reason, he will be quick to tell you that she is finding fulfillment elsewhere.

This jealousy is created because the abuser is insecure in the relationship. He has no faith in his own attractiveness to his woman and reacts to the subconscious thought that the one he loves may choose someone else over him. Ironically, his jealousy may eventually create the situation he fears most. She may indeed leave him to find someone else more caring and sensitive.

The real tragedy is that the abuser is doing the only thing he knows how to do. He is reacting the only way he knows to react—physically. Deep inside, he knows that something is wrong and he fears the worst. Unfortunately, his fear is self-perpetuating and will probably be the cause of his worst nightmare.

2. Need to Control

An abusive person has an overwhelming need to be in control. He is not the type to ask for help from anyone, especially his wife. To her, he must present himself as the "real man" who has all the answers. He does not allow her to have much input into decision-making, and is likely to reject any advice that she offers.

This desire to be in control is not the same as with a person who is simply a natural born leader. In the case of an abusive person, he doesn't just *prefer* to be in control, he *must* be in control. There is no room for questioning his authority. This would be considered mutiny from the one he loves. Any insubordination is responded to with anger and often severe abuse. He becomes a dictator, demanding total obedience.

But a dictator, unlike a king, is hated. A king gives time to the betterment of his subjects, sponsoring charities and events to benefit those in need, helping them to maintain their freedom and independence. He is most often loved by his subjects. In sharp contrast, a dictator usually controls his subjects and rules with an iron hand, forcing them to do his bidding or face horrible consequences. He does not want them to be independent or free. And he is most often hated.

As with the jealousy, this need to control stems from insecurity. The abuser often has a low self-esteem, and as long as he is in charge, he can feel important. This is a way for him to bolster his self-image.

Somewhere beneath the cruelness of the domination is what I believe to be real love. I know that I truly loved my wife. But it is not a love that we control. It is a love that controls us instead. The closest illustration to this kind of love that I can think

As with the jealousy, this need to control stems from insecurity. The abuser often has a low self-esteem, and as long as he is in charge, he can feel important. This is a way for him to bolster his self-image.

of is that of a small child loving a baby bird— squeezing it so hard that the bird is hurt or killed. The child really loves the bird, but he cannot see how his actions are destroying it.

So then, jealousy and a need to control will characterize the behavior of one who is prone to abuse. But if these behaviors are so strong, why is it that many abusive relationships go unnoticed? The answer to this is that the abusive person only exhibits these characteristics when he feels threatened in his relationship in some way, and it is only with her that he expresses his dissatisfaction. And that usually happens when they are alone.

If he is not feeling threatened, an abuser responds very normally to the world around him. This is the reason that an abusive person can be, like me, a pillar of his community. In my case, I was a strong Christian during most of my years of abuse to Ginnie. I not only went to church, but I was a deacon and had seminary training. I spent most of the free time I had involved in church-sponsored activities.

This is also why when I was not angry at Ginnie,

we had some very good times. We played together as a family and experienced many happy moments. No one outside of our immediate family even knew of the problems that we were having. Our friends did not know. My mother still does not believe it. We were the perfect little family as far as the world was concerned.

I was never the kind of person who got irate or mean at work. I almost never got agitated at my fellow workers or friends. I didn't get angry with my brothers or sister, my neighbors, or anyone else— only my wife and children. And I went to great lengths to keep anyone outside of my immediate family from finding out what was going on behind those closed doors.

To accomplish that, I used to threaten Ginnie and my children, too, that if they told anyone there would be worse trouble for them. It's almost as if there were two completely different sides to me—I was Dr. Jekyl and Mr. Hyde.

The saddest part is that as I acted out the O.J. Syndrome, I did not even realize what I was doing. Like the child who squeezes the baby bird to death and then wonders why it died, I wondered what was wrong with my relationship. I never saw that the real problem was my own possessiveness and abuse. Instead, I was trying to change Ginnie.

This problem is not relegated to marriage alone. Abuse of women is prevalent in relationships whether marriage is involved or not. In today's "society of singles," that's an important point. I believe that the issue of abuse may be deeply related to the fear of

19

> **Like the child who squeezes the baby bird to death and then wonders why it died, I wondered what was wrong with my relationship.**

commitment seen in our society and shared by men and women alike.

For me, the abusive behavior is all in my past. Let me tell you how I changed and how my marriage finally became all I ever dreamed it would be.

- 2 -

Bitter-Sweet Beginnings

My wife, Ginnie, and I both attended the same high school—Lake Worth High School in Lake Worth, Florida. When I was a senior, she was a freshman. I didn't know her then, but I well remember the first time I noticed her. I was going upstairs to class one day when a girl ahead of me on the stairs tripped and fell on the landing between floors.

The girl not only spilled her books and notebooks but her dress went up around her head. It was the day of bobby socks, penny loafers and full, ankle-length skirts. Girls didn't show their legs very often back then. Perhaps that's why I remember best those legs that went all the way up to her white panties. I helped her pick up her books, she thanked me, and that was that. Little did I know then that one day she would become my wife and lifetime companion.

The next time I remember noticing her was at the gas station where I worked the summer after graduating from high school. I was earning money to go to Palm Beach Community College near where I lived. Ginnie's parents often came to the station for gas. My

21

dad also worked at the station and one day when she was just leaving he said, "If I were your age, I'd go after that one." After that I started looking for her.

In the fall I worked up the courage to go over to her car and talk to her while her parents were inside, intending to ask her out on a date. My hands were wet from nervous perspiration, but, surprisingly, the conversation came fairly easily. Still, I couldn't seem to find the courage to ask her for the date. Her little brother was also in the car and must have noticed my nervousness and hesitation, because he blurted out, "Why don't you ask her out?" I did and she accepted.

For our first date we went to the high school football game, and right from the start there were signs of trouble. It became obvious that we didn't agree on very much. I was a long, long way from realizing how different men and women are. I was simply attracted to her physical beauty and didn't think about the rest. I don't believe I even knew that there was anything else to be concerned about.

I have often looked back on my early years and wondered why we weren't taught about things like relationships in school. Along with being taught how to read, write and think in today's society, we also need to be taught how to live with each other.

I discovered much later that we learn that from our parents or other adult role models. Boys learn how to relate to women from their father or whatever dominant male figure is the leader in their early lives, and they generally follow his example when they begin to form their own relationships with the opposite sex. For me, the role model was my father.

My father was a good man. He had been married before he met my mother—something I didn't know until long after I was grown. I have two half sisters whom I have never met. His divorce was so nasty that not only did his ex-wife hate him, but the two girls turned against him as well.

My mother was different. It was her first marriage and she was 28 while he was 42. Perhaps it was this age difference that made her so willing to accept his authoritarian ways. However, he did have a lot of other redeeming qualities.

I can't say I had a bad childhood, and only now as I look back do I see the abuse my father put my mother through. It wasn't physical as far as I know, but it could have been. Mostly he was verbally and emotionally rough on her. He often cut her down and put her in her place in front of my siblings and me. He was unmovable when it came to getting his way. But my mother never let on while he was alive how unhappy she was in the relationship.

When my father died in 1979 my mother became a new person. She was so full of life! At the time I didn't understand it and I resented it. I became afraid that Ginnie would feel the same way when I died. I was angry with Ginnie for something that had not occurred and that I would not be around to witness if it did occur.

I believe the reason I reacted to this situation

with such fear was that subconsciously I knew that I was treating Ginnie as badly as my father had treated my mother and even worse. I was doing what I had been taught to do. My mother put up with it, but as I was to find out, Ginnie would not for very long.

During our dating life, Ginnie and I fought and made up on a regular basis. It came naturally to me and I never questioned the fact that we disagreed so much. I remember well the first time I became jealous. The week after our first date, Ginnie went out with someone else. I was furious. I guess she didn't understand yet that she belonged to me. We had only had one date, but I was already building that prison of jealousy around her.

But that was only the beginning of the problem for me. I never seemed to be able to trust that she would not find someone else, or that someone else would not find her. It manifested itself even in small ways, like the time Ginnie got mad at me and tore up a love note she had written to me. I made her rewrite the note, exactly as she had written it before. I still have it after nearly 40 years. In a way it gave me a sense of security to have something in writing that promised she would love me forever, as silly as that may sound.

After a stormy courtship that lasted about a year, Ginnie and I got engaged. By then she was a senior in high school while I was a sophomore at college. What we had in common was our strong physical attraction for each other. Other than that, there was really nothing holding our relationship together. In the beginning we were both pretty crazy. We would spend long hours

**Our wedding day.
Ginnie had no idea what kind
of husband I would turn out to be.**

"making out." We fought constantly, but I was not truly abusive yet, at least not physically.

Then, on February 22, 1958, we were married. Neither of our families nor our friends thought it was a good idea, but we did it anyway. (One thing we shared was our determination and self-will.) We had fought

25

almost every day over that year and a half courtship.

Ginnie became pregnant right away after we were married, probably on our wedding night. Many of our friends and family were suspicious of how quickly this occurred. Back then it wasn't OK for women to become pregnant before they were married. But Ginnie and I had made a conscious choice to wait until after we were married to have sex, so we knew that their suspicions were unfounded.

Our life together had a pretty rough start. I had just quit my job, she was still in high school and pregnant. We were both teenagers, living in the attic above my parents' house. We couldn't agree on anything. This would have been a rough start for the best of couples, and we were not the best of couples.

For me there was the chemistry. I was strongly attracted to Ginnie in every way. For Ginnie there was chemistry too, but it was slowly being neutralized by my behavior. I couldn't get her to listen to me or to have sex the way I wanted to. I bullied her but she resisted, so I became more physical, often beating her head against the bed or wall. When I look back now I can't imagine why I did that—in fact, I don't remember it all that well.... but she does.

It must be a terrifying ordeal for a young woman to come to the realization that her "Prince Charming" or "Knight in Shining Armor" is in reality becoming a raging monster who will not only fail to "take her away from it all to live happily ever after" but may instead kill her himself. And, if he doesn't kill her, what

---

It must be a terrifying ordeal for a young woman to come to the realization that her "Prince Charming" or "Knight in Shining Armor" is in reality becoming a raging monster who will not only fail to "take her away from it all to live happily ever after" but may instead kill her himself. And, if he doesn't kill her, what meaning will her life have if she is dead inside?

---

meaning will her life have if she is dead inside?

In less than 4 years we had 3 daughters. Just before Marie, our second daughter, was born, I became infatuated with another woman. I even went so far as to send her roses. Somehow Ginnie found out. During the huge argument that followed, I told Ginnie I wanted a divorce. We had only been married a little over two years and I was already talking about ending it, which would have been the biggest mistake of my life. We talked about the divorce several times, but never took the steps to do anything about it.

The truth was, we really didn't know what to do. We were both unhappy in the relationship, both knowing that this was not the way it was supposed to be. I blamed it on Ginnie, as abusers tend to do. It simply couldn't have been my fault. All she had to do was to submit to me and do what I wanted and everything would have been great!

Then we heard about a Billy Graham crusade in West Palm Beach. We decided to go, partly out of curiosity and partly because I realized that something in our lives had to change. Marie was only a month old and Ruth, our oldest, was almost two. We took them both because we couldn't afford a baby-sitter. Secretly, I hoped that this religious meeting would make Ginnie see the error of her ways and decide to submit to me.

I don't remember what Dr. Graham talked about, but when he gave the invitation at the end, I told Ginnie we should respond. She was already a Christian, but she agreed to go down to the front with me anyway. All four of us went and I prayed with a counselor. I was not really sure if I should feel any different after the experience, and I was not really expecting anything significant to happen.

Something did happen, however. Instead of the meeting changing Ginnie, it had changed me. I felt like a new person. I no longer wanted a divorce. I wanted to make my marriage work. I can't explain what happened or why I felt so different, but even my friends and family noticed. They all wondered what had made such a change in me.

The next two years after that were some of the happiest we have had in our marriage. I loved Ginnie more than I ever had before. It was during this time that we decided to have another child.

But even though I felt so different inside, I was still abusive to Ginnie. It wasn't so frequent and perhaps not so violent, but it was still there, and as before, most often it revolved around sex. I wanted to be intimate more often than she did, and I was not willing to accept no for an answer when she wasn't in the mood. I screamed and ranted until she gave in, and if that did not work, I would get violent in order to persuade her. I always won, but it was an empty victory.

- 3 -

More Signs of Trouble

I got a good job and during those next two years we bought our first home, but I wasn't content. Something still wasn't right between us. We were still fighting, and I had a growing sense that I was losing Ginnie. This was confirmed one day when I came home unexpectedly and found Ginnie kissing another man, a mutual acquaintance of ours, in our home. She swore nothing serious was going on between them, but it was obvious that she was attracted to him. It was more than I could deal with rationally, and my jealousy escalated almost beyond control.

It wasn't until many years later that I learned that one of the results of jealousy and abuse is that the abuser's wife will often seek out and find another man. Instead of looking to me for comfort and intimacy, Ginnie began to seek it elsewhere, with someone she could trust not to treat her with such contempt.

By treating her the way I was, I was creating what I feared most. The more jealous and abusive I was, the more she pulled away from me. And the more vulnerable she was to the attentions of another man.

We were so young and in love. Neither of us was ready for the responsiblity of a family and the tension that would bring to our marriage.

But I couldn't see what was happening.

With this incident in the back of my mind, I decided we should move to Ft. Worth, Texas so I could continue my education there. I wanted to make sure that Ginnie was far away from any temptation. So we sold the house, loaded up our family, and left for Texas to start what we thought would be a new life.

Our arrival in Ft. Worth was heralded by the hottest temperature on record for that day. Despite the

One of the results of jealousy and abuse is that the abuser's wife will often seek out and find another man. By treating her the way I was, I was creating what I feared most. The more jealous and abusive I was, the more she pulled away from me. And the more vulnerable she was to the attentions of another man.

heat, we were determined to put the past behind us and make this our home. We quickly settled in, and I began going to school during the day and working at night in order to pay the bills.

It had been six years since our last daughter, Karen, had been born, and Ginnie and I did not plan to have any more children. We knew we couldn't afford to have any more. What we didn't know, however, was that after a certain period of time using the same birth control medication, a woman's body chemistry may change, making the medication less effective. This is what happened in Ginnie's case. Although she was faithful in taking her pills, she became pregnant anyway. So along came our only son, Tim.

Meanwhile, I had met a woman at work—"Cathy"—a young, married woman and the mother of a small baby. Her husband treated her badly, so she was looking for love, and the two of us hit it off. A friend of hers had played matchmaker in getting us together. It was a highly emotional affair, a relief from the constant fighting in which Ginnie and I were engaged.

The relationship never culminated in sex, but Cathy made it clear that I could have done anything I wanted with her. It never dawned on me that Ginnie was just as vulnerable as this woman was because Ginnie was looking for love, too. I was too blinded by my own need to be loved to see her pain.

I believe that this tendency for an abusive male to become interested in another woman is another part and indication of the problem. I understand perfectly how those two things go together.

I was looking for another woman who would respond the way I wanted Ginnie to respond. It wasn't that I didn't love Ginnie. It was that I wanted the control that she wouldn't give me. I imagined that in the fantasy of a new relationship, all of what I was missing would be found. But the reality is that no woman worth having would have given me what I was asking for—total control over her life. She would have to have been a slave or a possession.

It didn't take long for me to break off the affair with Cathy. I knew it wasn't right and would lead nowhere. Fortunately, just as Tim was about to be born, the company I was working for at night asked me to move to Delaware with them. They were shutting down the plant in Texas and offered me a good job plus moving expenses if I went. I had not yet gotten my degree, but I realized that it would probably be better for my marriage if I left the area, so I took the opportunity.

We waited until a week after Tim had been born to make the move. I alone had relocated to Delaware a few weeks before, which meant that I wasn't there for the birth of my son. Ginnie found this hard to forgive.

I went to work on the third shift again. This meant that I had to do most of my sleeping during the day. With three children and a baby in the house, this was almost impossible to do. I held Ginnie responsible for keeping the children quiet while I tried to sleep. And I took it out on her if my sleep was interrupted.

We were the model family on the outside, but day by day our relationship got a little worse. I was unhappy and Ginnie was miserable. The kids kept to themselves and comforted one another. When Ruth became a teenager we discovered that we had a built-in baby-sitter. Going out without the children gave us an opportunity to fight in private.

A lot of the time, we fought over sex. Ginnie had been very passionate before we were married, but that was before we actually had sex. I was into men's magazines, and I had certain ideas about what I wanted to do. Ginnie resisted these things, saying they made her feel like a whore. I didn't understand her point of view, and I pushed the issue. Sometimes I would get very rough. I thought that if I insisted strongly enough she would see things my way, but that never happened.

To quote a line from the butler in *Dangerous Liaisons,* "It's easy to get a woman to do what she wants to do, but it's getting her to do what I want to do

> "It's easy to get a woman to do what she wants to do, but it's getting her to do what I want to do that's giving me a headache."

that's giving me a headache." It was giving her a headache too. Since I thought I was right and I knew that I was supposed to be the boss, I didn't care that she didn't like it and I didn't care that it took brute force to get what I wanted.

Somewhere during this period, Ginnie began to fight back. She had decided that I was not going to abuse her without a struggle, even though she knew that I would win any physical contest. She had moved past the point of caring about our relationship. Now she was fighting for her children.

But getting what I wanted in this manner usually left me with an empty feeling that sucked all of the gratification out of the act. This in turn made me even more angry and I would become even more demanding. It was a vicious cycle that I could not seem to break. Why couldn't she just do what I wanted? After all, we were married. Why did she have to get me upset and cause all of those fights and hard feelings?

I knew what she was supposed to do—SUB-

MIT. That's what I wanted from her. It was what the Bible said she was supposed to do. But instead she just lay there like a prostitute, showing no feeling or emotion for me.

That scene was repeated hundreds of times over the first years of our marriage, and thousands of times over the first 22 years. But it wasn't always sex that caused problems. Often we would nearly come to blows over where we were going for a weekend or what we were going to do. Vacations were the worst times. We fought over where, when, what, and how.

I remember one of our worst fights. We were going into the Appalachian Mountains in Tennessee, headed for Florida to see our families. We had been discussing how we would handle the sleeping arrangements when we got there, since there wasn't really enough space at any one family's house for all of us to stay together. Ginnie wanted Tim and me to stay with my mother while she and the girls stayed with her mother. I saw this as a rejection of me, imagining that she only wanted to get away from me for a while. She saw it as a chance to get some peace and quiet for a change.

With our four children cowering in the back seat, we had a knock-down-drag-out fight in the front seat. Finally I stopped the car and told her to get out. The next thing I knew she was walking down the highway.

By this time, the kids were hysterical, crying into the pillows they had brought with them and praying fervently for us. But I didn't care. Ginnie was wrong and I wasn't going to give in.

I let her walk for a while, but in the end I asked for a truce. You see, I didn't really want to lose her, I just wanted to coerce her into doing things my way. Asking for a truce never involved admitting defeat. It was just a way to smooth things over for the moment.

> **Asking for a truce never involved admitting defeat. It was just a way to smooth things over for the moment.**

- 4 -

A Change of Venue Solves Nothing

When you're not really happy you want something, anything, to change. We weren't happy in Delaware and began thinking of moving to upstate New York. My company had a plant there and I wanted a transfer. We had prayed about it for a long time and had almost given up hope just before my boss made the offer.

Clifton Park is a bedroom community located 12 miles north of Albany. It is bursting at the seams with middle class houses, green lawns, trees, and children. We were sure that things would be better here than they had been before. We bought a brand new house for $45,000. It sat on a half acre of land and came with $450 a month payments. But best of all, there was a huge bedroom over the garage, almost like a dorm room, where all of the girls could bunk together.

Once again, our relationship seemed better for a while after the move. Ginnie had been working when we lived in Delaware, but she didn't get a job right away here, saying she would rather be at home. As time went by and I fell into my same old pattern of abuse, she became very unhappy, so I pushed her to look for work on the outside. I thought this would make a positive difference. In the end, it made things worse.

My new position at work was far more stressful than the old one and soon we were having fights that made the previous ones seem mild. I kicked in a door. I hit Ginnie. I was constantly angry that she wouldn't do what I wanted her to do, especially regarding our sex life. She even tried to commit suicide because she saw no way out. I can only shake my head in sorrow when I think that this is what I did to the woman I love.

Over the six years we lived there, the girls grew up. Ruth married a young man she met at college. Karen became involved with a boy in high school and decided to go to college in Arkansas, where he was going to go. Since he was two years older than she was, she worked it out so that she could graduate a year early from high school and go on to college that much sooner.

They may deny it, but I'll always be convinced that my children wanted to get away from home to escape the anger and fighting that characterized our life together. It almost makes me cry to think about it, but I have no one to blame but myself. I have to live with the reality of what I've done.

Our middle daughter, Marie, vividly recalls one time when she came in from playing to find Ginnie and me yelling in the kitchen. She watched as we ended up wrestling with each other on the floor, rolling around and cursing at each other. She ran out of the house and hid in the woods, crying and praying for God to somehow help us.

It wasn't until years later that I found out that such an experience was common for our girls. They often witnessed our fights, but never said anything to me about it because they were afraid of me.

Over those six years in New York, our marriage really deteriorated. Ginnie's solace was a good job at the VA Hospital in Albany. She worked in the psychology department and felt more at home there than at our house. Since she wasn't being warm and responsive to me, I was sure she was secretly seeing someone else. I had thought this many times before, but only that one time in Florida did I have any evidence to prove it.

One day I decided to go through her purse. It was not the first time I had done this. From time to time I had searched for something to support my paranoia that she was unfaithful to me. But this was the first time I found anything of interest. Ginnie had a love note in her purse.

If I had set out to write the note any man would least like to find in his wife's possession, this would be it, word for word. In it, she vowed her undying love to some other man and promised to wait for "him" forever, no matter how long it took. It said he was gentle, kind, and understanding. It said he really cared for her and she for him. And it made me nauseous.

It's very difficult to describe the feeling that I

got when I read that note. What I had feared most during my marriage had been confirmed. It was like having someone punch me as hard as possible in the stomach. Fear as strong as the fear of death welled up in me, and along with that came an overwhelming rage. I wanted to lash out, to hurt something. I was sure that the worst had happened, or at least was about to happen, between my wife and this man.

Under normal circumstances I would not have wanted Ginnie to know that I had been digging in her purse, but this kind of discovery I could not keep to myself. I was livid. I not only confronted Ginnie, but I put on a show that Jack Nicholson would have been proud of. I wanted to convince her that she was making the wrong choice. I hoped that by reacting so strongly, I could show her how much she meant to me. Typical of a person experiencing the O.J. Syndrome, I was doing irrational acts to achieve rational objectives.

Thinking back on that moment, I know exactly how a man can come to the point of killing the woman he loves. Whether or not he says it, he's thinking, "If I can't have her, no one will." In the moment of that passion, a man is not only capable of doing harm to someone, but he is super energized to take whatever action he allows himself to take.

My rage went on far into the night. That in itself was not unusual, since we'd had all night fights before, but the intensity of my anger was unusual. For 21 years I had tried to intimidate Ginnie and break her, but it hadn't worked. I didn't know what else to do.

> Thinking back on that moment, I know exactly how a man can come to the point of killing the woman he loves. Whether or not he says it, he's thinking, "If I can't have her, no one will." In the moment of that passion, a man is not only capable of doing harm to someone, but he is super energized to take whatever action he allows himself to take.

Nowhere in my mind during this fit of rage was the incident where I had sent roses to the girl in Florida or the time I had been passionate with Cathy. This was different. The shoe was on the other foot and it hurt like hell! It was put on with a sledgehammer, not a shoehorn.

I must have been one scary, pathetic person.

A few days later I came home to an empty house. Ginnie had gone to a friend's house to stay. She had sent our daughter Marie to Florida to visit my mother-in-law, and had Karen and Tim with her. Ruth was away at college at the time. I was still trying to take in the fact that she was gone when the phone rang. It was our pastor.

He started the conversation with, "I received a call late last night from Virginia and she told me about the problems you are having." It took me a moment to get over the shock of his knowing about our private life because I had always been convinced that what we did at home was no one else's business. My eventual response to his statement was to curse him out and slam down the phone.

I was angry, resentful, and scared all at the same time. My thoughts bounced back and forth like a rubber ball between blaming her and blaming myself for the situation, but I knew I would never admit to her that I might be wrong. I was afraid that she might never come back. I was angry that she would have so little respect for my position as husband and head of the house. I could hardly eat or work. At night I would pace the floor until I was exhausted and fell asleep.

After about a week Ginnie called me and said she wanted to come over and talk. Of course I agreed. The meeting was tense and I was angry again, but I didn't want to live without her, so I agreed to try harder and meet with our pastor for counseling.

We went to counseling a few times, but it only created more turmoil, mostly because the pastor told her that she should submit to me. It was music to my ears, but it only made her more resolute. We eventually stopped going altogether. Divorce became a regular word in many of our heated discussions, but we went on with our miserable marriage instead. Marie came back in about a month from her visit with my in-laws and before long our family was back to what we had always known as normal.

Let me say at this point that we did have some good times in our marriage. There were days when we laughed together and the veil of abuse and anger would

**Ginnie and I with our family.
Despite the abuse, we did have
some happy times together.**

temporarily be lifted. During these times of respite I
would remember what it was that attracted me to Ginnie in the first place. She can be so full of life. But
these times never lasted. She would say or do something that I didn't approve of or refuse to do something
I wanted her to do and we would be embroiled in our
anger and my abuse once again.

- 5 -

The Beginning of an End

Not long after Ginnie left me for that week, I was offered another position with my company in northern California. Ginnie didn't want to go and I suspected it was because she didn't want to leave her "friend." She denied this and suggested I go ahead by myself. I refused to leave her there with him.

We had many late night sessions in which I pushed her to go, but she kept resisting. She would have vesting at her job in only a few weeks and was reluctant to give that up. She also didn't want to take Tim out of a good school where he was doing well. And we had finally lived in one place long enough for her to develop friends that she didn't want to leave. I didn't care about any of these things.

I just kept pushing until she finally agreed to go with me.

As everyone knows, houses don't come cheap in California. The job I got was in a town just north of San Francisco called San Raphael. We couldn't come close to affording that area, so we ended up buying in a little town called Petaluma, 40 miles to the north. It's

Ginnie at one of the worst points in our marriage. Even though she had always had a very trim, beautiful figure, she became so depressed that she put on about 20 pounds.

two claims to fame are arm wrestling competitions and the production of eggs.

We couldn't find a good church and Ginnie didn't look for a job. I don't know what she did all day, but in the evenings we would often fight. It was obvious that something was going to have to happen in the relationship, but I ignored all of the signs. We frequently talked of suicide—both of us. My work was more stressful than ever and the hours were longer as well. Tim was having a hard time in school. Marie, the only daughter who was still living with us at the time, was working at a bank.

February 8th is Ginnie's mother's birthday. In 1980 it was also a Friday. I had talked with Ginnie on the phone around noon and everything seemed fine then. But when I came home from work about 6 pm and her car wasn't there, I got the feeling that something was wrong.

Tim had just come home from playing at a nearby school and Marie was not yet home from work. I asked Tim where his mother was and he said he didn't know. I went into the bedroom. It seemed unusually empty, but I wasn't sure why. A paralyzing fear began to grow in the pit of my stomach. I began looking around, and the realization that she had left slapped me in the face when I found that her suitcases, clothes, and other personal items were not there.

Frantically I looked for clues as to where she might have gone. In a waste paper basket I found a bank statement showing an account I knew nothing about. There was also a receipt for a private post office box, but I found nothing else to indicate where she was headed.

For the first time in our relationship, I didn't get angry. This time instead, I became severely depressed. I was sure she had gone back to New York to be with her "friend." I thought about going there and killing both of them. If you ask her, she will tell you that she believed that if I had caught her with another man I would have killed them both. That's the "O.J. Syndrome" at its worst.

I began making phone calls to everyone I thought she might contact, especially friends in New York and her family in Florida, but if any of them knew where she was, they wouldn't tell me.

I called my boss and told him I wasn't coming back to work. Then I called a realtor to list the house for sale. I also called an auction company and asked them to sell our furniture. It felt as though my life was over. It was only two weeks short of 22 years since we had made that commitment for better or for worse, and I guess much of it had been "worse," at least for her. It hadn't been that great for me, either.

To my relief, Ginnie went to Florida instead of New York. I rented a trailer, took Marie to live with some friends in New York, and Tim and I went to Florida with what was left of our belongings. I hadn't had any communication with Ginnie since she left, but I had talked with her mother, which was how I found out where she was staying.

If you ask her, she will tell you that she believed that if I had caught her with another man I would have killed them both. That's the "O.J. Syndrome" at its worst.

I quit a very good job to salvage my marriage. My boss said he understood, but I'm sure he didn't. Anyone who doesn't share my problem of abuse can't possibly understand what drives us to do the things we do. We just have to be in control.

I kept wondering who I could blame for the mess I was in. It certainly couldn't have been my fault. I was the husband. I was supposed to "wear the pants" in our relationship and be the head of the house. I wanted to blame Ginnie. If she would just do what I wanted her to do and think what I wanted her to think, there wouldn't have been a problem. At that point, it never occurred to me to blame my father or, heaven forbid, myself.

So, what was wrong with my being the dictator and Ginnie being the subject? That's how my mother and father acted. A woman's job is to submit to her man, isn't it? These were the thoughts that were running through my mind. I found myself crying much of the time, becoming lethargic and consumed with anxiety.

The O.J. Syndrome

When Tim and I arrived back in Florida, I rented a storage space for our belongings and found an apartment. I got a job—lower level supervision. Finding a top level management position in manufacturing was all but impossible and besides, I wasn't emotionally up to it anyway.

Meanwhile, Ginnie had gotten a job herself and moved into her own apartment. At first, she would have nothing to do with me. She wouldn't even talk to me on the phone. When she finally did consent to have a conversation with me, via telephone, of course, she said she would never, never live with me again no matter what I did or said. The only reason she would talk to me was because she missed Tim and wanted to see him.

One of the things I had wondered about was why she had left Tim with me. She was an excellent mother and I knew it was unusual for a woman to leave her children whatever the circumstances. Her answer cut straight through me. She said she was afraid to take him because she thought I would hunt them down and kill them both. If not that, she thought I might kill myself, and having Tim to take care of would keep me from doing that.

At this point, I began trying to figure out a way to use Tim to get her back. It's not that I didn't love my son. It's just that conquering Ginnie was more important to me. Nothing else seemed to matter. We who abuse are consumed by our passion and we lose all sense of what's right and what's wrong. It may not make any sense, but it's all part of the O.J. Syndrome.

Ginnie began going to a therapist and so I decided to go to one too in hopes that it would lead to our reunion. The woman I chose had been a therapist for many years and came highly recommended. I asked if she could get Ginnie and I back together. "No problem," she said.

When she finally contacted Ginnie to try to arrange a session with the three of us, the whole thing blew up in the therapist's face. Ginnie told her in no uncertain terms that she wasn't interested in meeting with her. She claimed that the doctor was only interested in the money that she was getting from me and not in the fact that I was an abusive husband. I never went back to the therapist after that.

Meanwhile, Ginnie's counselor told her that if she went back to me, she would only leave again. Ginnie also counseled with a local pastor who told her to get as far away from me as possible. As a result, she became doubly convinced that it could never work and swore openly that she would never live with me again.

Over the next few weeks I saw her only rarely, often just from a distance. I remember the time I saw her in a laundromat where she had gone after an aerobics class. She looked incredible, and I knew I couldn't go near her. It seemed almost surreal that I couldn't even approach the woman I had lived with for 22 years.

Ginnie was determined to file for divorce as soon as the six month Florida waiting period expired. I was sure that she would divorce me and then move back to New York to be with her secret friend. The whole scenario chilled me to the bone with a kind of mind-numbing fear. If that happened, I wasn't sure what I would do, but I knew that I would not stand by idly and let it happen. I was capable of anything at this point.

She wanted to spend time with Tim from time to time and I agreed, mostly because it gave me a chance to see her. I could see that there wasn't much change in her attitude, so when she asked if Tim could go with her to Disney World, I said yes. Secretly, though, I planned to use Tim to get back at her. I was still trying to pressure her with whatever means I had. I waited until the last minute when she called to say she was on her way to pick him up and told her that I wouldn't allow him to go.

With that one act she reacted like a knife, severing all contact with either of us. We had been separated for two months, and all indications were that our life together was over.

It was then that I decided I should explain to Tim that his mother was not coming back, even though we had been praying that she would. I explained it to him as best I could, trying not to upset him more that I had to. He was almost 13 years old, so I thought he was old enough to handle the truth.

At first his reaction was typical. He said he knew that Mom was coming back to us. I explained again the unlikelihood of this and told him that I didn't want him to be disappointed by getting his hopes up too high. I tried to tell him that we would do just fine on our own, but no matter what I said, he just kept insisting that she was going to come back. Finally I half-heartedly asked him how he could be so sure of her return. I was grasping at straws for any glimmer of hope. Maybe Tim knew something that I didn't.

I never could have expected his answer.

Tim told me that he knew Ginnie was coming back to us because he had a dream. You see, he had prayed one night and asked God to bring his mother back to him. That night he dreamed he was walking along a beautiful street when a voice spoke to him. He didn't see anyone, but the voice said, "I've heard your request and I will send your mother back. I will speak to her on May 2nd. Be patient and you will be a family again."

On May 2nd Ginnie would come back to us, he was sure.

Prophetic dreams were something that I had little association with in my life, so I was skeptical of Tim's revelation. Nevertheless, he was my son, so I tried to be supportive. I cautioned him again about not becoming too hopeful, but he continued to staunchly profess that she would come back on May 2nd. I finally let the subject drop, and neither one of us mentioned it again.

May 2nd came and went without any fanfare. I was a little disappointed when it did because a small part of me had hoped that Tim's prophesy would come true. I was careful not to make an issue of the date to Tim, however, hoping that he had forgotten.

The O.J. Syndrome

On May 3rd I got an important-looking envelope in the mail. It was from my realtor in California. I had not been able to sell our house in Petaluma before I left, and it had finally sold. The envelope contained the papers to be signed for the sale of the house.

This gave me the opportunity to call Ginnie and perhaps even see her, since the papers had to be signed by both of us. I knew that we could sign them separately and that this is what Ginnie would probably want to do, but when I called I asked her if we could meet at the office of a notary and go in together. To my surprise, she agreed, and we set up a time and place to meet the next Saturday.

It was a long, anxious week for me. I couldn't wait to see her. When I arrived at the appointed spot she was already there waiting. I pulled up, parked nearby, and she got out. But instead of heading toward the door of the notary, she walked straight over to my car and got in. We cautiously exchanged formal greetings and then she said, "I have to talk to you." I was a bit surprised but eagerly told her I would listen. I was still hoping for a miracle.

I never could have imagined what she said.

Her story went something like this: "Last Friday night I was talking with my mother and sisters, telling them I would rather die than go back to you. I meant it and I still do, but I have to come back to you."

In my shock, all I could think of to say in response to her statement was, "Why?"

She continued, "When I went to sleep that night,

God woke me up almost immediately and told me as clearly as I'm talking to you now that I have to go back to you. Even though I believe I will die if I do it, I have to do what He says."

I asked her to tell me on which Friday all of this happened. It was Friday, May 2nd. She knew nothing of Tim's prophecy, so when I told her about it she was a little encouraged. I was ecstatic.

Her one request was that we wait till her birthday on July 1st to move in together. That would give her a little time to get used to the idea and would give us both time to find a larger apartment. Neither hers nor mine was big enough for the three of us.

At that point I looked forward to what I thought would be the best day of my life. Five long months would have passed, but we had our whole future yet to live. I don't know why I thought things would be different this time. They never had been before.

Many times when couples split up they go back for a second try. Ginnie's counselor had told her that she would only leave me again if she came back, but I refused to think about that now. I didn't want to think that was possible.

We rented a two bedroom apartment and moved in together on July 1st, one happy family again. At least, that's the way I wanted it to be. The reality was that we were all nervous. I didn't know how to act or what she wanted me to do. She asked if we could wait a while before having sex, and I reluctantly agreed. In my mind, everything was back to the way it should be.

Why wait? In her mind, she still wanted to be away from me. No real healing had taken place. I didn't want to admit it, but we were both very uncomfortable in this "new" relationship.

We decided to buy a house so that we could have more room. Ginnie seemed cold and withdrawn most of the time, especially when we were close physically. I'm not sure it was all that different from the way it had always been before, but now I seemed to notice it more. I was constantly afraid that she would leave again. All of my energy went to trying to keep from getting angry with her. I didn't want a fight, and I knew that if I hit her again she would never give me another chance.

Before long, a friend from work called me and offered me a job back in California. After I had quit, he had moved on to another company and was determined to get me back out on the West Coast. I told him no at first, but he kept calling and finally I agreed. I decided it might be good to go back to the part of the country where our worst problems had occurred, sort of like getting right back on a horse after falling off. Besides, the offer was very good and we were struggling to make ends meet in Florida.

So, after a year and a half, we were on the move again. The house we bought in southern California this time was our sixth house and it was our 14th move since we had gotten married. This time, only Tim was left at home. Marie had gotten married—a small ceremony in our home in Florida.

The O.J. Syndrome

The new job was interesting and it paid well, but it also came with the characteristic stresses that affect life at home. Where I had been walking on eggshells with Ginnie, I soon started to break a few. It worried me that our relationship seemed to be moving backward, but I couldn't seem to do anything about it. As before, I prayed a lot about the problem, but it didn't seem to help. Our relationship crept back to where it was before she left as surely as the noonday sun slips onto the horizon. And as before, I felt helpless to do anything about it, in spite of my resolve.

At times I would try so hard and manage to go two, maybe three days without blowing up at her. The ugly subjects of divorce and suicide began surfacing in our altercations again. After three years, it seemed inevitable that one of those two would happen. We had some of our worst quarrels on the way to and from church, something which made Ginnie more distant than ever. She questioned my spirituality and my faith. So did I.

In front of friends and the rest of the world, we were a happy, loving couple. In front of God and in our own eyes, we were a miserable failure.

In the summer of 1984, about four years after we moved in together, I came to the end of my rope. I gave up trying and gave up praying about my marriage. With my best efforts, I could only go two or three days without getting angry and blowing up at Ginnie. I felt like even God couldn't help me. I lost all interest in going to church. The situation seemed hopeless.

57

The O.J. Syndrome

We had slowly and agonizingly made the emotional trek back to the same place we had been when she left. I began to think that perhaps the counselors were right—we were just too different to make it. Tim was almost grown and it would soon be just the two of us in the house. That in itself was a sobering thought.

Sometimes I wonder why we endured so much pain for so long. Two less determined people would have given up long ago. We were so different, and perhaps it would have been best for each of us to find someone else.

- 6 -

The End of a Beginning—My Second Marriage

A few times in a person's life, there are moments that are significantly memorable— moments in which the entire course of a life changes in an instant. These moments can't be planned, and they are usually unexpected. But when they occur, they remind us that miracles can happen.

Saturday, August 18, 1984 was to hold that kind of wonderful, life-changing moment for me. It was so simple, yet so profound.

Ginnie and I were at home alone. Tim was off playing somewhere and Ginnie was in the kitchen cooking something—hamburgers, I think. The day was typical for southern California—hot, heavy air that smells of pollution and stings your eyes and throat. I had wanted to go to the beach and have a picnic, since the ocean air is so much fresher, but Ginnie wanted to stay home and get some work done. She worked a full time job during the week and weekends were her time to catch up on her second job, housework.

We had already had words about whether or not to go, and I was not about to let the issue drop without pressing it. I marched into the kitchen intending to demand that she go along with my suggestion, reasoning that I worked hard all week and I should be able to go to the beach on the weekend with my wife if I wanted to. In my mind, I quickly brushed aside her reasons for not wanting to go. I could feel the anger starting to take over my mind. This was the way I had always gotten what I wanted in the past. I needed to be in control.

But this time something totally unexpected happened. I heard a small voice inside me say, "You are a man. You are stronger than she is. Why don't you just put your feelings and needs aside and listen to her? You can do it. You don't have to get angry, and what you're about to blow up about isn't really that important anyway. Her feelings are more important."

When I started to speak, the words caught in my throat and I couldn't say anything. A scripture verse popped into my head. Without saying a word to Ginnie, I swallowed hard and went to the bedroom to get my Bible. Keep in mind that I wasn't going to church at this time and I wasn't even praying. This small voice that spoke to me came out of the blue.

I had read Ephesians chapter 5 many times in my life. I had become proficient at preaching to Ginnie the part in verses 22 through 24 that tells a woman that she ought to submit to her husband. It was the scripture on which I had based my perception of marriage for all of those years.

This time, however, what caught my eye was

verses 25 through 30. Suddenly it all seemed so simple.
I could not have realized at the time how much that one
moment of enlightenment would change my entire life
and my marriage from that day on.

In case you don't have a Bible handy, let me quote
the scripture that I read that day.

> Husbands, love your wives, just as Christ
> loved the church and gave Himself for her,
> to make her holy, cleansing her by the wash-
> ing with water through the word, and to pres-
> ent her to Himself as a radiant church, with-
> out stain or wrinkle or any other blemish, but
> holy and blameless.
>
> In the same way, husbands ought to love
> their wives as their own bodies. He who loves
> his wife loves himself. After all, no one ever
> hated his own body, but he feeds and cares
> for it, just as Christ does the church—for we
> are members of His body. For this reason a
> man shall leave His father and mother and be
> united to his wife, and the two shall become
> one flesh. Ephesians 5:25-30.

I had read those verses a thousand times in my
life, but only now did I understand what they really
meant. I had been trying to be the head of my wife by
being her ruler, her dictator, but I was supposed to be
the head of my wife by laying down my life for her like
Jesus did for the Church. In other words, I should put
my wife's feelings and priorities before my own. The

command the Bible gave to me was not to demand respect but to earn it by giving up my own way. I had to die inside.

While I sat there reading and rereading these verses, trying to digest the truth of what had finally illumined me, Ginnie came into the room. She realized right away that something was different about me. She had been expecting a tirade from me over her unwillingness to go to the beach, but it never came. She wanted to know what was going on, so I told her about my experience. I explained that I knew now that in order to love her I had to lay down my life for her.

She had never heard me talk this way before. I knew that she would have trouble believing that I meant what I was saying to her. She had suffered for so many years my abuse and demands, and she had watched me try to change so many times, only to see me fail again and again. It was hard for her to accept that I would change now.

But I did change.

For the next few weeks and months I worked hard at it. Each time I wanted to demand from Ginnie that she do what I was asking her to do, I remembered those verses and that thought came into my mind again, "You are a man. You don't have to get angry Her feelings are more important than yours." It was there, and I couldn't ignore it.

I had to literally bite my tongue on many occasions. My goal was to show her that she was more important to me than I was to myself, and so I yielded

I explained that I knew now that in order to love her I had to lay down my life for her.

to her wishes and desires. I discovered during that time how important Ginnie's feelings were to her, and so I began to try to respond to those feelings rather than my perception of the situation.

Before, I had wanted to assert my manhood. I had wanted to prove that I was stronger than she was— that I was a real man. Now I realized that getting my own way was the easy way out. I could always out-bully her. But to out-love her took all of the strength that I had.

What I had previously focused on in the Scriptures was that part in Ephesians 5:22-24 that tells women what to do in relation to their men. That is where I found the now famous word "submit." After this life-changing experience, I realized that those verses were not addressed to me. They were written to her. They were not my concern. In a way, I had been playing God, trying to get Ginnie to submit to me while totally ignoring my own part, what I was supposed to do.

Since man was created first, I believe he must do his job first in a relationship. Then and only then can a woman do hers. It just doesn't work the other way. I see many examples of that every day, and my own father and mother were prime illustrations of that fact for me.

Ginnie and I on our 35th wedding anniver-
sary. I never knew how beautiful it could be
to be loved by her until I stopped thinking of
myself and began to love her the way I always should have.

> I had been playing God, trying to get Ginnie to submit to me while totally ignoring my own part, what I was supposed to do.

If Ginnie were to have submitted to me in what I was demanding, we could never have had a meaningful relationship. It would have been like a master and his slave. I can clearly see now that the situation would not have been satisfactory for either of us. I guess God knows what He is doing after all.

What I began doing was not a "Yes ma'am"— "Yes dear" type response, but rather a powerful, will-driven kind of love that puts another person, specifically your mate, first, before your own needs. Real love is kind, thoughtful, yielding, long-suffering, hopeful, giving, quiet, and gentle, and it is the act of our will.

No woman wants milk toast for a man. Men in this situation are not happy and neither are the women who rule over them. I did not lay down my authority but rather my need to control and have my own way. I laid down my need to be a dictator. Now when Ginnie says something, I evaluate it and make a decision based on what I know, giving heavy weight to her input because I know she is very often right.

Giving up my own way, laying down my life, is the job for a "real man"—not what I had been doing before.

The O.J. Syndrome

It became obvious to me that I had never regarded Ginnie's feelings as being important. Feelings to me were secondary to facts. But to a woman, her feelings and emotions are inextricably tied to her inner self. By ignoring her feelings or scoffing at them, I was rejecting who she was inside. Laying down my life for her meant putting her feelings first before my own wishes and desires.

At first Ginnie was not responsive to the "new me." She was suspicious and hesitant to trust that the change in me was permanent. To trust me now and be let down one more time would have destroyed her. So she was cautious.

But eventually, over time, she began to respond. I had always wanted her to love me in an intimate, exclusive way. I had always wanted her to believe in me and look to me for advice or comfort. Slowly she began to do just that. For nearly 30 years I had been trying to change her and get her to do what I wanted. Now, because I was putting her feelings first, she was doing all of that willingly.

It was amazing to watch this unfold. Like a butterfly coming out of a cocoon, our relationship was transformed in those months following my revelation until now, at last, we have a love affair.

There are so many differences in how we relate to each other, but I'd like to share three of them that I consider the most important, those which are of primary importance to me.

First and most importantly to me as a man, our

> Like a butterfly coming out of a cocoon, our relationship was transformed in those months following my revelation until now, at last, we have a love affair.

sex life has become what I always dreamed it would be. Ginnie is now warm and loving toward me. Instead of forcing her to make love to me, she does it because she wants to and often she is the one who initiates it. She never did that before. How incredible it is to be loved back by the one you love!

Secondly, she now comes to me for guidance and decisions, even those that relate primarily to her. For all of those years I was her dictator, demanding that my decisions be law; I was in control only because she feared me. But now I have earned her respect, and I feel like a king because she has made me a king. I wanted to be in control, and now I am more than ever before because she trusts me. She wants me to make decisions for us.

Thirdly, my spiritual life has changed 180 degrees. I am thoroughly convinced that how I treat my wife directly correlates to how well I can fellowship with God. How could I truly love and follow Him when I was abusing my own wife?

The O.J. Syndrome

Since the time that all of this happened, I have discovered two warnings in the Bible, both directed at the man and not the woman, and both with consequences for not heeding them. I believe these warnings are for every man, no matter what his beliefs.

According to Malachi 2:14 in the Old Testament, men who treat their spouses as badly as I did should not expect God to accept their worship or their offerings. And according to I Peter 3:7, if men don't honor their wives, God won't hear their prayers. No wonder my spiritual life had reached rock bottom.

One of the first things I did after my marriage was restored was to tell a friend at work about it. He diagnosed me as being in need of a special place to worship. As I said, my spiritual life had gone so far awry that I hated going to church and had even stopped praying before the transformation occurred in my marriage.

My friend suggested the Church on the Way in Van Nuys which was at least 35 miles from my home in Thousand Oaks. He likened the church to a spiritual "hospital" and said it would be worth the trip. I decided to try it.

Our first visit was an amazing experience for me. The church is charismatic, and having been Southern Baptist for 25 years, I wasn't used to people raising their hands to worship. I also wasn't prepared for the overflowing of warmth that I had never before experienced in a church. I cried tears of joy.

From that day, my spiritual life, like my marriage, became transformed. I couldn't wait for Sunday and Wednesday so that we could go to church. Before, I had hidden my true self from other church members, covered by a cloak of secrecy about my home life and spiritual life as well. Both had been in shambles and I did not want anyone else to know.

Now, I saw and heard people sharing their deepest thoughts and problems with others. And I saw the caring and supportive way they were treated. Soon I was doing the same thing. Abuse, the crime of secrecy, can't survive in the light of openness. Just as burglars and rapists often seek the dark of night to hide their crimes, abusers wait for the "darkness" of their homes to commit their injustices.

It is the way the church responds to that openness that really matters. In other churches I would no doubt have been the subject of gossip and condemnation, but not there. When everyone shares and everyone cares, it works to promote healing. Transparency, letting others know what is going on in the deepest part of my life, has replaced the secrecy of my abuse.

The Church on the Way helped to bring my problem into the light of day. It gave me a chance to grow and be supported and encouraged as I worked to make my marriage all that it should have been. It also gave me a chance to help others by sharing my story. Before, I couldn't even help myself. I am thoroughly convinced that every church has the God-given responsibility to promote transparency and provide the setting in which it can flourish.

The O.J. Syndrome

What was born on that hot August day in southern California has continued to grow and mature in me. I won't pretend that their haven't been difficult times, but the abuse has stopped. As time has passed it has become more and more an instinctive reaction in me to put her feelings first. I wouldn't trade anything for the relationship we have now. It's getting stronger every day.

I was thinking recently about the story of the Beauty and the Beast. There are some parallels in that story to the one that occurred in my life. The Beast is a fearful, ugly person until he becomes willing to die for the Beauty. Only then does he become the prince she always dreamed of loving.

This is exactly the way I found it to work with Ginnie and myself. Until I was willing to die for Ginnie, i.e. to lay down my priorities in favor of her feelings and priorities, I was a beast to her. Only when I gave up myself did I become her true "Prince Charming."

Now, I automatically tune in to her feelings. I can't always follow her reasoning process, but I can listen to what she is saying she needs or thinks should be done. Her instincts are usually right, and I am all the richer for having listened.

- 7 -

Suffer the Little Children

I have told you the story of my abusive marriage as though Ginnie and I were the only players in this script. Unfortunately, our children were players as well. They were witnesses and unwilling participants in all of the abuse and anger. And they suffered for it as well as Ginnie and I did.

Consequently, no book about my abusive marriage would be complete without the children's point of view, and that's what this chapter is all about. I have asked each of my children to tell in their own words their thoughts and feelings on what it was like growing up with abuse and, since they are all grown now, how that abuse has affected their life as adults. As you will see, each of them has suffered in his or her own way. And each of them learned to cope in his or her own way as well.

Ruth—

What I remember most about my early childhood is fear—fear of Dad's temper and his fits of rage.

I was in terror whenever he got mad. I remember once he was mad at me and I got so scared that I went and hid in the basement. I could hear him calling for me upstairs, "Ruth Ann!" over and over. He would always use our middle names when he was angry with us. But I refused to come out. I just couldn't face his wrath. I hid until he forgot about me.

Living in terror of my dad's temper all of the time made me decide that I would never let myself get out of control that way. I purposefully went in the opposite direction and hid all of my feelings. I don't remember feeling happy, sad , or angry as I grew up. I felt nothing. That way I was always in control. That way no one could really hurt me.

But my lack of emotion began to have its effects on my life. I found once I became an adult that I couldn't be truly intimate with my husband. Since I wouldn't allow myself to feel, I didn't know how to share what was deep inside of me. I didn't even know myself what was deep inside of me. It had been so long since I had explored my own feelings that I had forgotten how.

I also developed a basic mistrust of men. My father was my only male role model, and since I couldn't trust him, I couldn't trust any man. Even if I had been able to feel my own emotions, I probably wouldn't have shared them with my husband anyway because of this mistrust. I had to come to the place where I could begin to feel again before I could begin to trust again. And that was a long, hard road I would have to travel.

One other result of growing up watching my dad

treat my mother the way he did was that I automatically assumed certain roles in my own household. My dad had very clear role definitions that he imposed on our family. My mom did all of the cooking, cleaning, and taking care of the children, even though most of the time she had a job as well as he did. But when Dad came home from work, he would eat dinner and then relax for the evening, while Mom still had work around the house to do.

In my house, I do all of the same things that my mother did. I don't ask my husband, Jim, to help because a part of me deep down thinks that wouldn't be right. The housework is my job. It would be disrespectful to ask him to help me out. I know in my head that it doesn't have to be this way, but my subconscious mind won't let me change. It's almost impossible sometimes to shake off your past.

Marie—

I don't think I would be as close as I am to my sister Karen if all of this hadn't happened. We needed each other and knew we would always be there for each other. We shared all of the emotions possible over the years.

I am insecure about my relationships with men. I feel that they all look down on me and I'm not worthy or good enough to be their friend. I have a hard time relating to them. The main reason I fell in love with my husband, Randy, was that he was such a positive person. He was always building me up by saying that I was pretty, nice, terrific, etc. Coming to someone with low self esteem, that was heaven.

I feel insecure in my relationship with my parents. I feel like I have to behave a certain way or act a certain way or they will look down on me or maybe not like me as much. I don't feel that I can be totally honest with them about some things for fear that I will hurt their feelings.

One positive thing that came out of my upbringing is that because of all of the fighting, I was determined to have a better family life with my own children. I have striven to give my children a secure, happy home where they will always feel loved and safe. I tell them that they can tell me anything and I will always listen, even if I don't agree.

I am a very strong willed person. I think that it has definitely worked to my advantage in my marriage (sometimes). Mom let Dad push her around and control her for years and years. First of all, I didn't marry a domineering person like my dad was, and second of all, I don't let myself be pushed around.

Lots of times I think that Mom and Dad were so wrapped up in their marriage together and all of its traumas that they didn't notice what was going on with us kids. I pretty much picked all of my high school classes without their knowledge or input. I know they trusted us a lot, but maybe they shouldn't have (at least me).

I know Mom and Dad loved us a lot. They were always concerned with our problems when we told them. Mom made me many dresses for my performances and they always came to our recitals. But they were too wrapped up in their own problems to really be there for us. I miss that.

Karen—

It's funny how children see their world sometimes. I, too, was scared of my father's fits of rage and terrified of his anger. But I never blamed my father. Instead, I idolized him. I saw him as the man who could do anything. Through all of the abuse I watched him heap on my mother, I never thought he was a bad person. He was my hero, and I desperately wanted to please him. I became a perfectionist in order to do so. I thought if I could just do all of the right things he would love me, and I needed so desperately for him to love me.

The horrible part of all of this was that I blamed my mother for my dad's behavior. I thought that she could change the way my dad acted by being nicer to him and showing him a little more respect. If she would only love him, he wouldn't get so mad. I know now what hell my mother went through and how hard it must have been for her to even tolerate the whole situation.

Unfortunately, I also thought that if I didn't do the right things, he would stop loving me. I grew up believing that love was a fragile thing that could be taken away at any moment if I wasn't careful. And this feeling bled over into all of my other relationships as well. I was constantly trying to please everyone else, and I spent many hours hating myself if I thought I hadn't said or done the right thing in a certain situation. I never felt secure with anyone's love. I was sure that their love depended on my earning it by acting the way they would want me to act. It has only been in the last few years that I have worked through this fear of rejection and learned to be myself.

But the biggest regret that I have in all of this is that my parents were absent from my life as I grew up. They were so wrapped up in their own hurts that they couldn't reach out to us. Dad was angry much of the time, so we would all try to stay out of his way lest he turn his anger on us. And Mom was there physically, but emotionally she left us. She had to in order to survive. She couldn't deal with Dad's abuse and give 100% of herself to her children at the same time, so we never really had those deep talks that mother and daughter are supposed to have. I felt detached from her and Dad both.

Tim—

When I heard that my dad was writing a book about how he abused my mom, I was shocked. I never saw my dad abuse my mom. I knew they fought, but don't all couples? And most of those fights were behind closed doors, so I never really knew how bad they were. I remember hearing shouts from their bedroom and the sound of something banging around in there, but I just thought it was another argument and they would work it out.

Now that I know about the abuse, though, I wonder if the tendency to abuse is genetic. I can get so enraged at my wife. I bottle everything up until suddenly I explode and lose control completely. Sometimes I scare myself with how angry I get. We have some pretty big fights, and sometimes we even get into shoving matches. I'm always sorry afterward, and we make up, but I can't seem to control the anger.

I have never understood why I am so insecure in my relationships, especially with my wife. I know I'm possessive, jealous, and overprotective. I need to be in control all of the time. I'm always afraid that I will lose her, and so I want to know where she is and what she is doing at all times.

Now I can see that I am acting just like my dad did with my mom. Maybe it's genetic. Or maybe I picked it up without realizing it by living every day with them and watching how they acted. Perhaps in the back of my mind, I grew up thinking this was the way it was supposed to be.

Our children before they were all grown. They seem happy, but how does my abuse still affect their lives?

- 8 -

Phases of Love
Ackerman's Theory

I am convinced that some of how Ginnie and I related to each other, especially how I felt about her, has to do with the chemistry of love. By this I mean actual chemicals in the body that all of us have which affect emotions and actions in humans. You have probably noticed that some people seem to have a stronger attraction to the one they love than others. Today we are finally beginning to understand what makes that attraction. In a day of rampant drug abuse it's perhaps ironic that natural drugs are responsible for strong feelings that can lead to hurt and even death.

According to Dr. Diane Ackerman in her book *A Natural History of Love*, love is more than psychological. Dr. Ackerman identifies no less than three chemicals produced by the body that affect our emotional love behavior.

The first she identifies is Oxytocin, the "cuddle chemical." It is somewhat responsible for a lot of what we call "mother's love." It encourages labor contractions and plays a role in breast feeding, causing nipple erection and milk flow. She goes on to say, "...it seems

79

to play an equally important role in romantic love, as a sexual arousal hormone that prompts cuddling between lovers and sweetens pleasure during lovemaking."

Secondly, there is PEA, which Dr. Ackerman calls "the infatuation chemical." She says, "When two people find one another attractive, their bodies quiver with a gush of PEA, a molecule that speeds up the flow of information between nerve cells. An amphetaminelike chemical, PEA whips the brain into a frenzy of excitement, which is why lovers feel euphoric, rejuvenated, optimistic, and energized, happy to sit up all night or making love for hours on end."

But what happens if one of the partners does not share in this "chemical feast?" It could be that an abuser is on a PEA high while the one that he loves is not. In this case he may react like a drug addict who is deprived of a fix. He will do almost anything, including kill, to feed the addiction. This does not excuse his behavior, but it does help explain why making the relationship work is so important to him. He will do anything to keep it from ending. About 3/4 of the women who die from abuse each year die while trying to leave their abuser.

Dr. Ackerman goes on to say that research shows that PEA can be neutralized by something called MAO inhibitors. The use of these antidepressants will restore a lovesick person to normality. It appears that in some cases, due to an attraction, the brain is actually bathed in PEA and if the subject is rejected, he will go into a savage depression which, without an antidepressant, will only be reversed by falling in love again.

I believe that this PEA generated behavior is strongly tied to abuse, especially abuse that leads to injury or death.

The third chemical Dr. Ackerman calls "the attachment chemical." After infatuation subsides, a new group of chemicals takes over. These are morphinelike opiates of the mind which calm and reassure. "Being in love is like a state of chaotic equilibrium." The rewards of intimacy, dependability, warmth, empathy and shared experiences trigger the production of the mental comfort food, endorphins. "It's a less steep feeling than falling in love, but it's also steadier and more addictive."

But an abusive relationship never gets to the endorphin or "attachment chemical" stage. There can be no true intimacy, dependability, warmth, or even true empathy.

Intimacy is defined as "belonging to or characterizing one's deepest nature." While I was an abuser, I didn't know what the word meant. I heard people talk about it and figured it was something I was missing. I had the gnawing fear that Ginnie was having an intimate relationship with someone else. In the emotional sense of the word, she certainly wasn't with me. That made me even more jealous and dissatisfied in our relationship. I didn't realize how important emotional intimacy was for a person's well-being.

- 9 -

Men vs. Women
How Are They Basically Different?

To better understand abuse, we must learn more about the biological makeup of men and women. Men and women are not just different because they are brought up differently; they are born with some striking genetic differences as well. When these differences are understood, they can enhance a relationship, creating a fullness that is not there with one person alone. It's like working a jigsaw puzzle and putting all of the pieces in the proper place. When it's done, it all fits beautifully.

But if the puzzle isn't put together properly, there is a jumble of confused parts with little purpose or interaction. I believe that men and women are not meant to be the same but rather they are meant to complement each other, to fit together, and form a meaningful, working whole. Otherwise, the problems spill over into our society and our children.

One of the major differences in men and women has to do with a difference in their brains. In order to understand this dissimilarity, you must first understand a few basics about the brain itself:

The human brain is divided into two hemispheres, the left lobe and the right lobe. Connecting these two lobes is a set of dense fibers called the corpus callosum. The left side of the brain controls functions that are sequential such as logic and reasoning, math, and verbal skills. This side of the brain is linear and organized. Everything has a place and an order. Everything makes sense.

The right side of the brain controls functions that are more creative such as art, music, emotions, and imagination. Instead of being organized, it is spacial and holistic. Not everything has to make sense here. Imagery is important, and perception rather than facts is the basis of reality.

The corpus callosum in between these two halves of the brain allows interaction between the two lobes. Without it, the thought processes in each side of the brain would be isolated.

Research has discovered that the corpus collosum in a woman's brain is much more dense than in a man's. For this reason, a woman has much more interaction between the logical side of her brain and the creative side. This accounts for what many people call "woman's intuition." Her emotions become linked to any logical thought she may have. In fact, because of this connection, it is difficult for her to do anything without at least some emotional involvement.

For me, this has become the key to understanding Ginnie. I now realize that her emotions are an integral part of who she is, and that everything she thinks is tied to those emotions and feelings. If I want her to love and trust me, I must recognize her feelings as being important, not just some quirk of nature that made women difficult to deal with.

Similarly, I have learned to respect the intuition Ginnie sometimes relies on for decision making as being a valuable asset to our relationship. Before, I would brush this off as flightiness or lack of reasoning power. I can see now that this tendency to rely on intuition is not a drawback for her; rather, it is a powerful tool for both of us. Her intuition gives me a kind of second sight—a chance to see things from both a factual and an intuitive point of view. And it gives me knowledge and understanding that I could not have apart from her.

- 10 -

Kinds of Abuse

Abuse is defined as "improper treatment, a deceptive act, physical maltreatment, or abusive language." Webster also says that it "implies the anger of the [abuser] and suggests defamation and consequent shame and disgrace." Abuse has many faces and not all of them are violent. Yet all of them are a form of death for the victim.

Mental Abuse—

The simplest form of persecution is mental or emotional abuse. It is the quiet way to destroy someone you love. Ignore her, be totally disinterested in whatever her interests are, hold back your own feelings and thoughts, or act as though her feelings are inferior to your own and you are abusing her the same as if you had hit her.

This kind of abuse is harder to recognize than the others because there is usually no anger involved. There is only apathy. Take the example of "Stan" and "Beth."

The O.J. Syndrome

Stan was a successful accountant and a good, church-going man. Beth was a school teacher with aspirations of becoming a song-writer. They rarely fought, and everyone thought they had the perfect marriage. Underneath the facade, however, Beth was miserable.

The problem was that Stan never took an interest in what Beth wanted to do. He rarely showed any emotion at all toward her. He did not even seem interested in sex. Beth felt that Stan looked down his nose at her emotions and discouraged her from following her dreams. He often pointed out that she needed to live in the real world rather than pursuing a fairy tale. He didn't care about her feelings, only his own. Eventually, they developed two separate lives while living under one roof.

No amount of beating or screaming at her could have made Beth feel less loved than she felt when Stan ignored her. She wanted so badly to be loved but instead felt totally rejected.

"Susan's" case is very similar. She and her husband never fought, but he did not seem to care about what went on in her life. "Bob" worked long hard hours earning a living. They had three of the most beautiful little girls you have ever seen. On the outside, they were a perfect family, very active in church, excellent parents. Bob was successful in his job and a deacon at the church.

On the inside, however, their relationship was a disaster. Susan confessed that they had not ever had an argument in their married life, but that Bob was not interested in what went on in her life at all, perhaps not interested enough even to create an argument. She, like Beth, felt neglected. He wasn't interested in her feelings or her priorities, only his own. And she eventually found someone else who would care about what she did. Most of their friends never understood why she was so unhappy. They could not see how Bob was killing her on the inside.

Unfortunately, this kind of abuse is often missed. It is hard to recognize a problem when there is no violence, no anger. But a lack of love, a lack of caring, neglect, can be devastating because instead of wounding the body, they wound the soul. And the soul may take even longer to heal than the body.

The bottom line is that this kind of abuse is the same as any other, more visible form of abuse. Like the others, the man does not care about the woman's feelings or priorities.

But even if you miss this form of abuse, it is almost impossible to deny the next three.

Verbal Abuse—

A second form of abuse with which we are more familiar is verbal abuse. This often involves yelling or screaming, but can also be done in a very quiet voice. It happens any time a person is cut down with words.

Verbal abuse is particularly effective if you do it while towering over her, flexing your manly muscles and screaming at the top of your lungs. It's even better if you can go on for hours and hours, especially if she has a job and you can keep her up late on a work night. I always thought this would force Ginnie to give in, but in the end I only created more hatred in her. If you wake up the children after they have been put in bed for the night, as I almost always did, that also helps. Pretty soon, she will be willing to do anything you say in order to get some peace in her life, even if that means giving in to your demands.

Just like mental abuse, verbal abuse harms the soul. Without realizing why, the abused woman slowly begins to believe all of the things of which she is accused by her husband. Over time, she thinks less and less of herself. In my incessant attacks on Ginnie, I succeeded in killing what she needed most —her self-respect and self-esteem.

Physical Abuse—

The third and worst form of abuse is often a last resort for the abuser, when all else fails. It is a response to frustration in not getting his own way. In a last ditch effort to make the woman submit to his wishes, he strikes her.

The pattern is usually the same: first a disagreement over some small issue, then anger and verbal abuse which may last for quite some time, and finally, when he sees that "discussion" will not get him what he wants, the use of force. This kind of abuse destroys any hope for a meaningful relationship whether the woman stays with her tormentor or not.

Surprisingly enough, an episode of physical abuse is almost always followed by a deep remorse on the part of the abuser. He is sorry for causing her pain and wants to make everything right again between them. This remorse is genuine.

Because physical abuse usually occurs in a fit of anger, it is rarely planned. Later, when the strong feelings have disappeared, he no longer sees the reasons he had for striking her, and he wants his misdeed to be forgotten. He contends that he did not mean to hurt her— that he just "lost his head" for the moment. It's as if he thinks that this sorrow over deeds done will make them go away. But it never does.

In some cases, the abusive man has been drinking or taking drugs, but, unfortunately, that is not always the case. I never drank or used drugs. If you consider substance abuse an excuse, I didn't have one.

Fatal Abuse—

Abuse that results in the death of another person is a result of deep passion. It occurs when the abuser becomes so emotionally frustrated that he loses all sense of reality. Rarely is there ever a conscious decision to kill. Rather, anger overtakes his logical thought processes and before he can consider the consequences, it is done. As in the case of physical abuse, the abuser is usually genuinely remorseful after the act has been committed.

The O.J. Syndrome

In my own case, on several occasions I had thoughts of killing Ginnie, but I never followed through. Sometimes it happened because I would become so angry that I didn't care who or what I hurt. Over the years, Ginnie became more combative with me and even began hitting me back when I would hit her. This only made me more determined to show her that I was the boss, which could easily have led to my fatally injuring her. Thankfully, it didn't.

Also, when Ginnie left me and I was sure that she had gone back to New York to be with her friend, I thought many times about killing them both. I wanted her to pay for the hurt she was putting me through. As I said before, seventy-five percent of women who are killed by the man they love are killed while trying to leave. If he can't have her, he doesn't want anyone else to have her either.

But even though it wasn't my doing, fatal abuse has touched my family. Ginnie's sister, Judy, lived in Ohio with her husband. They eventually divorced and her ex-husband received custody of their two children, probably because Judy had a drinking problem. She had received a genetic tendency for that from her alcoholic father.

Judy's life went downhill quickly after the divorce. She lost a good paying job and ended up moving in with a man that none of us trusted. Judy told us about how he would hit her and abuse her. In the end, Judy died of a brain hemorrhage. The police never investigated the incident, but all of us, her family, know that she was a victim of fatal abuse.

> Abuse in any form is a horrendous crime to another human being. Unfortunately, it exists more often than we know. Many women never realize that they are victims of abuse, especially if it is mental or verbal abuse. They may think that their man is just hard to live with. Many stay with an abusive man for years and years, thinking that it will get better with time.
>
> It rarely does, but thank God in my case it did.

- 11 -

New Beginnings

It would be of no value for me to tell you my story unless you also could do what I've done in your own relationship. This chapter will put into practical terms the cure for an abusive marriage and the way to start having a wonderful time with the woman you love. I just can't put into words how incredible it is to finally have a real, two-way loving, caring relationship and, most of all, to get rid of that horrible, ugly, green monster— jealousy.

In order for Ginnie and I to get to where we are now, there had to be a lot of healing of the deep emotional damage that is always created when you abuse someone the way I did. This takes time. In fact, it took several years for some of Ginnie's wounds to heal. Even now she does not want to talk about the past because it can still bring pain to her. You must realize when you begin to change your life that it cannot happen overnight! But it was well worth the time and effort I had to give.

There are three basic principles involved in this way of living. Within these lie the prescription for a

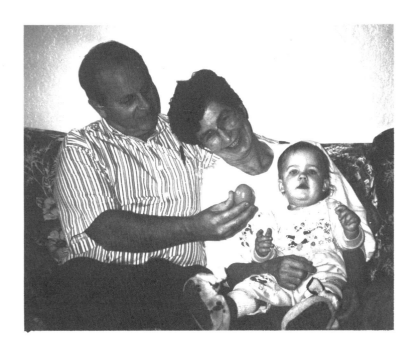

Ginnie and I with one of our 13 grandchildren. Emotional healing was a slow process, but time has helped. Now we can enjoy our life together and truly be partners in everything.

great marriage. If yours is already one of those great ones, chances are that you are already following these principles. If your marriage is less than what you hoped for, you probably are not.

I have set out these principles for the man, not the woman, in the relationship. The reason for this is that I believe that the man has the responsibility to love first. If he does, the woman will respond. It is nearly impossible not to love someone who is totally and unselfishly loving you. Our natural instincts cause us to return love given. If you think that you have been loving your wife and she has just not appreciated it, you will find once you study these principles that you have not truly been loving her the way she needs to be loved. You have just been doing what you would want her to do for you.

Let me add before I give you these principles one key element in changing the way you feel about your wife and the way she feels about you—in order for the transformation to take place, you must become selfless. We have all heard over and over that relationships are a 50-50 deal. That's not true. Relationships are a 100-100 deal. They are not give and take; they are give and give. To truly love someone else, you must give up yourself completely. One of the reasons your relationship has not been working up to this point is that you have been trying to get what you want out of it. But you will only get what you want when you first give what she needs and wants. I know this from my experience. Until I gave Ginnie all I had and asked for

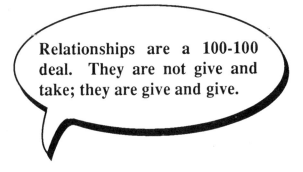

Relationships are a 100-100 deal. They are not give and take; they are give and give.

nothing in return, I never knew what it felt like for her to really love me. Now I do.

Principle #1: Lay down your life

At the very heart of any good marriage is a man who loves his wife so much that he is willing to give up his life for her. He is willing to put his feelings and priorities aside for hers. Make up your mind that this will be the number one priority for you. Most men would indeed put their lives at risk if someone else ever threatened their loved ones. But some men don't realize that they themselves are threatening their loved one's life and well-being.

But giving up your life isn't just a macho act of heroism like those seen on television. It is the daily decision that what is important to her is more important to you than your own desires. Be as selfish for her as you have been for yourself. Find out what matters to your wife and make those things matter to you as well. The returns are well worth what it takes to do this. This is what I now believe it takes to be a "real man."

For example, let's say your lady wants to go to lunch with some of the people at her office or with some friends in the neighborhood. And let's say there will be two women in the party and one very good looking man. If you are like I used to be, a red flag goes up. You don't think you can trust her with that other man. What if this one lunch is the beginning of a relationship for the two of them?

If you react as I used to and forbid her to go, you are not loving her. You must lay down your life and your desires for what will make her happy. If you don't, she will perceive that you don't trust her and don't care about her need to have friends. The next time she wants to go out, she probably won't mention it to you. By giving her your blessing, you keep the lines of communication open and you build her trust in you. You show her that her world is important to you and that you care. That is precisely what a woman wants and needs.

As another example, let's say you are on your way home with your wife one day. You decide to take the quickest route home, but she wants to go a different way. She doesn't know why. She just has a "funny feeling" that you should go another way home. Laying down your life for her means respecting this feeling as being more important to you than your own sense of what is logical. By listening to the "irrational" fear she has expressed and not taking the route you had originally intended, you build her trust in you as a person who really cares about what she thinks.

This principle is manifested most often in the little things. For instance, you occasionally rent a movie that you know she will like, but is not something you particularly enjoy. You have laid aside your own desires for something she would want. You may think this is too small of an act, but most marriages are made or broken on things much smaller than this. Put the toilet seat down after you use it. Clean up the kitchen without her asking for your help. Give the kids a bath before she gets a chance to. Find a million little ways of saying that you know what she wants and needs and you are eager to give her those things. I guarantee that she will notice and will respond with warmth and appreciation.

Principle #2: Her feelings matter most

This principle is often the hardest for a man to follow because, as we discussed in a previous chapter, men generally do not make decisions with their emotions, while women often do. Don't make the mistake of thinking that how a woman feels is not relevant. It is. Her feelings must be considered more important than yours if you want this to work. For many women, how they feel is the only relevant factor in making a decision. Learn to respect this way of thinking rather than condemning it as being irrational.

I find that many times a woman will have an objection to something her husband does simply on the basis of a feeling, not on the basis of any real facts.

This is not because she is being illogical. It is a woman's automatic response to the world around her.

Remember, the thicker corpus callosum in a woman's brain causes her to connect emotions with facts, and vice versa. She will always be more in tune with feelings and therefore, feelings are important to her. Men have to learn to accept this fact.

A woman's feelings are real to her, just as real as anything else in her life. They are not just something that happens as a sidelight. To truly love your lady, you must address her feelings as well as her thoughts. For example, when you are having a discussion with her, don't just ask her what she thinks about the subject. Ask her how she feels about it as well. Let her know that you care about this part of herself.

Another thing that makes this principle so difficult for some men is that men are often scared of a woman's emotions. They don't understand them and they don't know what to do with them. The best way to handle this is to let your lady know that you feel this way. Tell her you don't understand but would like to, and then listen to what she tells you. You will be surprised at how eager she will be to help you out when she perceives that you really care about her feelings.

A word of warning here—when you listen to what she tells you about her feelings, listen with an open mind and heart. Don't just listen to hear what you want to hear. She may have feelings that she has been holding in for some time because she was afraid to tell you about them. Be careful not to put her down for

> **Men are often scared of a woman's emotions. They don't understand them and they don't know what to do with them.**

expressing these to you. Just listen and be understanding.

Most of the time when women express fear, disappointment, or anger about a particular situation, they don't necessarily want the man they love to start giving them advice on how they should handle those feelings. What they want is your sympathy. They want someone to say, "I understand. I'm sorry. I love you. I'm here for you." It is so simple to give this kind of comfort, yet it is difficult for a man to resist the temptation to take over the situation and "fix it" for her. Don't give in to this temptation. Just listen to her feelings and respond with love.

Principle #3: Perception is reality

Each person that lives on this earth has his or her own separate reality. No matter what the circumstances that surround us, we each interpret those circumstances differently, and that becomes what is real to us. Two people may live in the same place, have the same type of family life, make about the same amount of money, and yet still one may be happy with his life and the other miserable. This is because the way we perceive our world becomes our world.

In a marriage relationship, if you love your wife with all of your heart, and yet she does not feel that you love her, for her the reality is that you don't love her. What you must do is to find out what it is that says love to her and do those things.

For example, you buy her flowers. You expect her to be surprised and pleased. Instead, she is angry that you wasted the money. In her mind, you have not shown her love. You have shown her that you do not love her because you are so willing to waste money that could be spent taking care of basic needs. It doesn't matter if you have all of the money in the world and you can convince her of this. It only matters that her perception is that you didn't care about her monetary worries.

Most of us have grown up with a mental image of what a loving relationship is. We imagine what marriage will be like and what true love feels like. We spend the first 25 to 30 years developing this picture. Then we get married and the person we love most does not act like the image we have in our minds. We become disillusioned. Sometimes this leads to the conclusion that the one we love does not really love us back.

When you find out what your wife's perception of true love is and what her image is of what married life should be, you can begin to show her how much you love her in ways that she will perceive as true love. You can begin to do the things that she thinks are loving, even if they are not things you would consider to be indicators of true love. If you do, she will begin to see you as her "dream man" because you are acting like the man she had envisioned all along. This is not trickery. This is giving her what she always wanted. This is loving her selflessly.

How do you find out what she considers true love to be? Ask her! Ask her what she expects and desires out of marriage. Talk about her dreams and what would make her feel truly loved. Most women are only too happy to tell you what they really want or need. But be careful to really listen to what she says, not to what you want to hear. It may be different than what you expect.

So then, these are the three basic principles to loving your wife. They will take every ounce of love that you have to put into action because they require you to totally give up yourself in the process. But they are worth the struggle to do because she cannot help but love you in return.

There are, however, some traps that men often fall into in trying to accomplish their goal. Here are four things to watch out for as you put the three principles above into action:

1. You can't fake it. Since women are so intuitive, they are very quick to see through an insincere person. If you don't really care about her feelings and are just going through the motions, she will figure it out very soon. Don't assume that she is that unaware and don't patronize her. You must truly love her and care about her for this to work.

2.No woman wants "Milk Toast." You have to be a man. If your responses to her are "Yes, dear" and "No, dear" she will not respect you any more than if you were demanding your own way. Giving her what she needs and desires is an active process of listening to her, setting aside your own priorities, and putting hers first. It is a proactive process rather than a reactive process.

This is a difficult thing for men to grasp. You must be strong while at the same time being sensitive. You must not be afraid to make decisions, but they must be based on what is best for your wife and considering everything she says. It is a delicate balance.

3.The woman is the judge of how well you are doing. Remember that her perception of the situation is her reality. If you have not gotten mad at her for several weeks and you think you are really putting her feelings first, but she thinks you haven't changed at all, then in her eyes you haven't changed at all. She must notice the change before it becomes real for either of you.

4.The woman makes the rules. Just kidding, sort of. It's very hard for a controlling person like me to get used to having someone else's input and priorities being a major consideration. I had to learn to let go of the reigns of control and allow her to know that her input had real, significant importance in our relationship. I had to learn to trust her as much as she had to learn to trust me.

If you follow the three principles outlined here and heed the cautions, you will begin to see a beautiful change in your relationship with the woman you love. When your actions allow her to see how much you care about her (and it is your actions, not just your words, that will make it happen), she will begin to trust you and open up to you in a way you have never seen before. If you have been really abusive, it may take a while for this to happen and you may have to swallow your pride many times. But it will happen.

You may also have failures and setbacks, as I certainly did, but keep on going and you will have success. Failures occur every time you get angry or abusive in any way and whenever you fail to consider her feelings. I know this from my own experience. When I tried to bully Ginnie into being what I wanted in a woman, all I got was pain and rejection. But when I put my own desires aside and just began to love her with all of my heart, she became all that I wanted her to be.

I remember a proverb I once read that made me furious. It is a common, well-known adage. Ginnie pointed it out to me quite some time ago, and at the time it enraged me because it contradicted the self-styled way I had been handling my relationship with her. Yet deep down I knew that there was truth in these words:

> **"If you love something, set it free.**
> **If it comes back to you, it's yours forever.**
> **If it doesn't, it wasn't yours anyway."**

I hated this proverb because I knew that if I set Ginnie free, she would never come back to me, so I clutched tighter. I tried to keep her near me physically while at the same time pushing her away emotionally. I knew that Ginnie wanted to be free, but I could not give her that freedom.

Back then, I would have preferred the version of this saying that I saw once on a bumper sticker, the version that could very well be an abuser's theme:

> **"If you love something, set it free.**
> **If it comes back to you, it's yours forever.**
> **If it doesn't come back, hunt it down and kill it."**

I'm sure that whoever made up that bumper sticker was trying to be funny, but for me it was too true to be funny. It is exactly what most abusers do to those they love. It was exactly what I was doing to Ginnie.

Ginnie often asked me, "How can I love
you if I don't trust you?" I didn't know
how to interpret that question. I wondered what love had to do with trust. I
didn't realize that love and trust are
almost the same thing. You can't have
a woman's love without first earning
her trust.

- 12 -

There is Hope

In all of my years of marriage to Ginnie, I always had two choices in responding to her:

1. Build up her trust in me.
2. Take over any situation through control and abuse.

It's easy for me to see now that only one of those actions could have improved our relationship and put me in the driver's seat. It took me twenty-six years to realize how important trust is to a woman and even longer to learn how to build that trust. It is a woman's emotional security in a relationship, and without it there can be no submission or giving of herself to another.

What Ginnie was silently saying to me all of those years when she resisted my authoritarian ways was that she didn't and couldn't trust me. She could not allow herself to put her life and well-being in my hands because I acted as though I did not care for her and her feelings at all. Every relationship starts with two people who are strangers, and instinct tells us that strangers are not to be trusted, at least not until you get to know them. And if you come to know them and realize that they do not have your best interests at heart, there is reason to fear rather than to trust.

I saw Ginnie's reluctance to trust as rejection of me, but it wasn't. Instead, it was her way of saving herself from the emotional and physical harm she received at my hands. She would only give so much of her inner self to me, reserving a large part that I could never touch and therefore never hurt.

I believe that almost any woman will naturally submit to a man who truly loves her, a man she feels she can trust. Now that I know this, I no longer spend my time fretting about why she doesn't want to do things my way. I no longer try to bully her into accepting my authority. There is no need for those things now, because now she trusts me. It is her own choice to submit to me. And it is my job to continue to lay down my life for her in order to be worthy of her trust.

In the back of my mind, I can still hear Ginnie's words of so long ago ringing in my ears: "You're a good man, Richard, but I just can't live with you any more." I don't ever want to hear those words again, and, thank God, I don't think I will have to. That way of life is in the past.

I won't pretend that Ginnie and I have a perfect marriage in all respects. We are still two very different people and we don't see eye-to-eye on many issues. But we are not the same two people who first met and fell in love either.

The O.J. Syndrome

In my learning how to really love Ginnie, we have been able to grow beyond what I hoped for, and we are still growing together every day. We are partners in our lives now. Even though I am putting her feelings and needs first, I believe that she outgives me.

Beyond that, I'm still amazed at how often Ginnie is right about what she feels and what she thinks we should do. Seeing her respond to me in such a positive way is reward enough for me.

One of the biggest lessons I have learned in all of this is that we need to be more forward-looking and visualize what we are becoming and what we are teaching our children by our actions.

That's what our pastor of the Church On the Way would call a "Tomorrow Person." He says, "Predecessors, plain people such as our parents, teachers or friends (even those disposed to our best interests) can cast shadows over our tomorrows.

They may have set boundaries on our lives, limited our view of ourselves or our potential. Or they may have been confined by boundaries of their own which found mirrored images in us. But in either case, our predecessors often shape us, leaving an imprint which may be the source of our own present frustration. How can we deal with this? Though God wants to free us into tomorrow, He won't allow us to blame yesterday. Neither will He allow us to cast blame on anything or anybody who seems to restrict our tomorrows."

I believe one of the main characteristics of being a real man is that a real man will stand up and take the blame for his actions. Sure, I could blame society, natural chemicals, physical differences in our brains, or my father for what I put Ginnie through, but if I want to be a "tomorrow person," I have to face the consequences for my own actions, whether they are pleasant or not.

I still have to stop and remind myself every once and a while that as a husband, I have a job and I alone am responsible for it. That job is to love my wife and lay down my own feelings in favor of hers. When I do that, life is beautiful for both of us. When I don't, no matter how hard Ginnie may try to correct my wrongs, life is miserable for both of us.

In spite of the imperfections, this life I now have is a universe away from the life threatening, depressing mess in which we were immersed for all of those years. At least now I know what to do, even if I don't do it perfectly every time. If I can help at least one more man see the potential or provide an answer for one who, like I was, is seeking a solution to his dilemma, then it will have been worth it all.

I have to believe that if I could turn it around after twenty-six years of abusive life, any man who really wants to can do it as well.

Epilogue: "I Don't Want to Remember"
By Ginnie Bean

Rich said he wanted me to write something for his book, but I didn't want to remember. I didn't want to think about that time in my life and the non-person that I was. I didn't want to think about the abuse and the sadness and screaming and utter aloneness. I want to remember only the good as we do when someone dies and we glorify them. I didn't want to remember.

I noticed him because he was cute; I watched him because he was my friend's brother and my friend obviously admired him; I learned a lot about him from my friend. My friend was his brother.

He was "older," a college man. I could look up to him. He was getting an education which was respected and valued. My parents said he would make me a good living. I was only in high school and was so flattered that he would notice me. I didn't know he would turn out to be so possessive and that the possessiveness would become a death grip later.

He wrote me love letters, extolling my virtues— which were my eyes, legs, the way I walked, the way I laughed, etc. I later burned those letters in a fit of hate. I liked his easy going laugh and his teasing manner. I didn't know he would later torture me with his teasing

110

and his laughing eyes would reflect the devil's soul.

He didn't scare me then. I was excited and, being young, confident that life was going to give me only a rosy future. He told me we were going to get married, I teasingly told him he had to ask but it wasn't true. He knew that he owned me already. It's funny how the female gender gives heart, soul, mind and body, but we expect to be loved, cherished, taken care of, valued. It wasn't to be, not for a very long time.

I remember our first disagreement after our marriage—the day after we exchanged our vows. Before our marriage I had set up an appointment to have a tooth extracted on the day after our wedding. I came home in pain and he yelled at me—he said it was because I had not planned it with him, but it was really just for hurting. I was crushed and later I was to realize that he couldn't stand to have me in pain and that it threatened him in some way. At the time I only knew that he hurt me. We were just married and in love, I thought. And so it began.

I remember the demands on my time, my attention, my devotion, my body. I was a living sacrifice to his desires, whatever they were, whenever he desired. I thought I was giving in to his whims because I loved him and he loved me and it was "the right and wifely thing to do." I know now I was insecure in what my role was and should be (I was only 17 at marriage and 18 when our first child came) and I was too naive to ask anyone. Later when the hurts really came fast and hard I wouldn't talk to anyone either because I was too

The O.J. Syndrome

ashamed of myself for allowing myself to marry someone who dominated me so totally and who, by his
actions, valued me for only one thing: physical pleasure. And I was too prideful to admit that we had done a
terrible thing to ourselves and to our fast arriving children. I couldn't let my family know I had made such a
mistake. He was demanding of my time, my attention,
"his" resources (income), my affection (even from our
children).

The years rolled along, some days happy and
reasonably contented. Most days were spent in a state
of exhaustion from taking care of the house, working a
full-time job, volunteering for a number of church positions, and "submitting to my husband."

We went to a Billy Graham crusade in West
Palm Beach and he accepted Jesus as his Savior and
changed. We started attending church on a very regular
basis, giving all we had in spare time and energy. Those
times were the most happy times of our lives together.

Our times at home when doing things with the
children were happy and fun. Our times at home alone,
locked in the bedroom with each other, were times of
demands and giving. However, I never gave enough,
never pleased the way he wanted, he said I didn't love
him ... and I began not to. But we had the children,
responsible jobs where everyone respected our wonderful family life, church positions of significant lead-
ership where we saw changes in others lives for the
better, and I still had my pride so I wouldn't talk with
anyone about any of it. He wouldn't talk with anyone

about any of it because he was "right," and his need to control was tremendous. After our involvement in the church and learning scriptures, etc. he used God's word to keep me in line. I guess he, through his haze of jealousy, saw me slipping away (mentally only at this point) and started clutching even more strongly to hold me to him. He was choking me. He made me responsible for his happiness and the burden was too great.

If I complained of pain in any form (emotional, mental, physical), I was told to shut up and enjoy "it." It was a living hell. In the early years, although we attended church on a regular basis and prayed to God for all our needs, I never prayed for our marriage. I just expected Rich to fix it. I expected him to be good, to love me, to cherish me, to take care of me and the children. But I found myself alone in a family setting, crying inside most days and crying outside some days from the pain I was in.

But I knew that he loved me—how did I stand the emotions that tumbled through my heart and head? Love, hate, fear, anger, hope, despair, protectiveness towards the children at all costs. I gave him children and then because he would threaten to use the children to hurt and control me, I gave them up completely.

The most wonderful thing I did throughout this time period in our lives was to give the children to God. I remember that night. It was another night of his demands, physical again. I had the three girls to feed, bathe, dress for bed, tuck in bed, etc. after I had cooked dinner and cleaned up the kitchen after working more than 8 hours that day. He could barely wait till the children were in bed before he claimed his rights. It was so degrading and I was crushed, totally spiritless. After he left the room I sobbed for a while out of pity and loneliness; and "cried unto the Lord." I knew that the girls could hear us shouting at each other in our unhappiness and I worried about them so. I remember in my despair asking the Lord to please take care of my girls. Those were the words I used, "take care of my girls." I had no idea as to how God would answer that plea. But I was totally incapable of anything at that point, as close to a nervous breakdown as anyone can be without going over the edge.

A few short weeks later in a church revival, one by one the girls came forward, requesting Jesus to come into their hearts. See, even though we live in the sewer, there is always a way for God to reach down and make something beautiful happen. And I praise Him because my girls and their families all love, worship and serve God to this day. I am eternally grateful for His answer to my plea. "Out of my distress...."

It hurts even now to think of all that we did to each other, mostly emotionally. We didn't build each other up. I still expected to be taken care of, cherished, etc. and waited for that to happen. I guess he expected me to respect and admire him but that was fast flying out the window. There were two things I admired in him during those stressful years: (1) his devotion to his children (after I emotionally stepped out of the picture); and (2) his devotion to doing God's work. You see, even in our most unpure state, we can serve God and have good results from all that we do. And I still admire him for that.

Five, ten, fifteen years sped by. The family picture was rosy: we were living the American dream—nice home, cars, good job, church-going family. The girls were excelling in school, outgoing and happy and had banded together many years before, therefore supporting each other through the terrible teen years. Our son, who had been born six years after the younger daughter, was "an only child." I know five is a lot, but I wish now I had a brother or sister for him! Wash my mouth out with soap!

And with the years and the success had come an almost total shutdown of my heart towards my husband. I had begun praying for God's intervention to change him, to change me, to fix us. But there was no answer, at least not one that we heard. I guess we were deaf—to God, to our children, to each other's spoken and unspoken needs. Our married life became rather perverted, not the loving supportive relationship couples are supposed to have, but one of taking and needing and desire and total dependency. And we were talking now, to counselors, but neither of us could get out of our pain long enough to see where the other one was.

Our son suffered tremendously during these years. He was largely ignored by both of us. I think he just grew up. And now, we all suffer the consequences—our son is unchurched, struggling with his own dreams and desires. I know God forgives us for our sins, but we will all suffer the consequences of them regardless. And in this instance I see the sins of the fathers visited on the children. God has forgiven me but I'm not sure I have yet. I cry even now because Rich and I were so involved with our own struggles with each other that we gave up those precious years with our children. Oh, we did enough with them. They tell me of the good things they remember, and I know they all love us and care about us and are very close to each other. But it could have been better! It could have been more fulfilling, rewarding and fruitful for all of us.

God did not intend for us to struggle with each other for all those years; He did not intend for us to turn deaf ears to His directions and blind eyes to the message we read in His Word. So you see we suffer the consequences, and part of that suffering is knowing that we hurt God by ignoring Him also.

When it all finally came to a head in 1980 (22 years in hell), I left. And I cried all across the country. I was so broken inside—why did I wait so long to leave? I left everything, including my children. Rich needed them more than I did (I thought to keep him alive) and I just wanted to escape the constant pain. So I finally ran home to Momma. I don't know what she thought, but she promised me it would all be all right (as mother's will) and prayed for all of us and shielded me from the barrage of phone calls that Rich made to her house.

In the shelter of Mom and Dad's home I began to recover a little, got a job, started receiving counseling. I remember the counselor told me that if I should ever return to the marriage relationship with Rich it would not last; I would leave again. I healed enough to move out of Mom's home, but I wasn't healed enough to deal with the hurts of our children, so I turned my back on them all and with a bravado to be proud of plowed ahead with my life.

But God wanted something different than I did. I remember waking up in my little twin bed in a disgusting little rented apartment and God speaking to me in a voice only I could hear. "You have to go back." And I cried.

But although I cried and knew without a shadow of a doubt that to return to Richard would be the literal death of me, I knew that I had to go back.

The emotions during those first few years back together were varied: anxiety, insecurity, fear; hope, timidity; hate, love (it never dies). Our son was with us still and he felt all these and more. I vowed never to run away to my parents again, not because of them but because there was no help for me anywhere. And I prayed, and tried to stay under the shelter of God's wing. I even remember during that time counseling another female friend to stay with her husband and she did and they have a lovely life together now. Life is complex.

But I was dying again. No self-worth, he took it away; I did not feel pretty (although he always said I was); no confidence in myself to do anything right. But one day it all changed.

117

He asked my opinion about something, I don't even remember what. But to give an opinion other than the one he already held was to challenge his authority and his wisdom and always started a fight. And the fights could never be side-stepped. He demanded participation. He would needle, scream, prompt until a reply was made; and then the injustice of it all would control me. But this time was different. I, knowing that I was about to speak "fighting" words, gave him my opinion (the opposite of his view). I was working at the kitchen sink and when I didn't hear the explosion, I looked around to see why not. We are really strange animals, aren't we? He was standing at the counter, clutching with his hands and clinching his teeth. And although we both felt the storm clouds gathering, there was no downpour. The first battle won!!

I didn't know at the time about his "deal" with God. But I saw the change. I felt the change. Gradually I was able to unfold my inner self, to open up and trust just a little. After a time he explained what had transpired between he and God and the changes that he was going through. All I can say is, "Praise God." Jealousy and possession are too much for any individual to bear, the burden far, far too great to stand. And my broken self, after Rich's change, began to heal and stand tall. I felt like a flower that's been rained on hard, blown by the wind, even stamped underfoot, that slowly reaches for the light when all the storms pass. And sends roots deep into the soil (God's heart) for stability and turns it's face upwards for nourishment and flowers in a beautiful way.

You see Rich not only abused me in his jealousy and dependency but he took away my trust in God. When Rich changed and started freeing me (as Jesus liberates) I began to grow and change too. When Rich changed and started to demonstrate his love for me, I began to return that love and to blossom in his love and God's love. No matter what we know of God's love, in a marriage relationship it is reflected in those we love. When those we love are less than they should be, it damages God's witness in the family. When Rich changed and allowed himself to be transformed truly according to God's Word, then the family was also transformed. Slowly at first but steadily towards the right path of deeply caring for each other, sharing our thoughts and needs in a good and giving way, supporting each other in whatever way is needed, and praying for each other on a daily basis.

I'm sorry for all the hurt that I endured. I'm sorry for all the hurt Rich endured (for although it really was his fault, he was still deeply in pain also). And, I am deeply sorry for the pain it caused our children. I am forever grateful to God for saving our children, for repairing the damage we did to each other, and for giving us another opportunity to support and help each other and our families and Christian friends.

Now can I forget again?

119

Bibliography

Entertainment Tonight . July 29, 1994.

Sylvia Ann Hewlett. "Tough Choices, Great Rewards". Parade Publications, Inc. New York, NY. July 17, 1994. pp. 4-5. Reprinted with permission from *Parade*, © 1994.

Ackerman, Diane. "Are You Made for Love?" Parade Publications, Inc. New York, NY. June 19, 1994. Permission from *Parade* and from author.

Holy Bible. New International Version. ©1973, 1978, 1984 by International Bible Society. Used by permission of Zondervan Publishing House.

For information packet on domestic violence, write: National Coalition Against Domestic Violence, PO Box 18749, Denver CO 80218-0749.

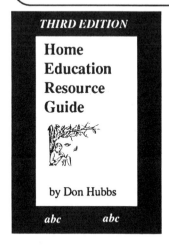

ROAD SCHOOL

by the Marousis Family

Many people dream, but few people pursue those dreams. Many hope for a better education for their children, but few do anything about it. This is the story of one family who did both.

In September of 1993, the Jim and Janet Marousis left Craig, Alaska, with $12,000, their pickup truck, and their daughters, Kaitlin, 10, and Jordin, 8. They began to "Road School" their daughters—and each other. This is the account of their adventures—of learning, changing, adapting, pleasures and disappointments.
ISBN 0-933025-36-X $14.95

Dr. Christman's Learn to Read Book

With just this one book, a person can teach anyone to read! It's true because people tell us about it every day! Here are some of the unsolicited comments we have heard at the office:

"I absolutely love this book!"—Carol Sanford, literacy volunteer at Aspen Prison.

"I teach as a volunteer for the literacy program. This book works very well. I am teaching a 60-year-old man who has never read in his life."—Mary Saxon.

"Best book for learning English ever!"—Tom Evans, asking to translate this book for use by Koreans.
ISBN 0-933025-17-3 $15.95

ORDER FORM

To order more books from Blue Bird Publishing, use this handy order form. To receive a free catalog of all of the current titles, please send business size SASE to address below.

_____Home Schools: An Alternative (3rd ed)	$11.95
_____Home Education Resource Guide (3rd ed)	$11.95
_____The Survival Guide to Step-Parenting	$11.95
_____Dr. Christman's Learn to Read Book	$15.95
_____Expanding Your Child's Horizons	$12.95
_____Parent's Solution to a Problem Child	$11.95
_____The O.J. Syndrome	$11.95
_____Road School	$14.95
_____Homeless! Without Addresses in America	$11.95
_____Green Earth Resource Guide	$12.95
_____Home Business Resource Guide	$11.95
_____The Sixth Sense: Practical Tips for Everyday Safety	$11.95
_____Under Two Heavens	$14.95

Shipping Charges: $2.50 for first book.
Add 50¢ for each additional book.
Total charges for books:_____
Total shipping charges:_____
TOTAL ENCLOSED:_____
NAME:_____
ADDRESS:_____
CITY, STATE, ZIP:_____
Telephone #:_____
For credit card order,
    card #:_____
Expiration date:_____

Send mail order to:
BLUE BIRD PUBLISHING
1739 East Broadway #306
Tempe AZ 85282
(602) 968-4088   (602) 831-6063